Therapeutic Exercises for Victimized and Neglected Girls:

Applications for Individual, Family, and Group Psychotherapy

Pearl Berman

Professional Resource Press
Sarasota, Florida

Published by Professional Resource Press
(An imprint of Professional Resource Exchange, Inc.)
Post Office Box 15560
Sarasota, FL 34277-1560

The copy editor for this book was Patricia Hammond, the managing editor was Debbie Fink, the production coordinator was Laurie Girsch, and Jami's Graphic Design created the cover.

Library of Congress Cataloging-in-Publication Data

Berman, Pearl. 1955.
    Therapeutic exercises for victimized and neglected girls :
applications for individual, family, and group psychotherapy / Pearl
Berman.
        p.   cm.
    Also includes: You sparkle : a handbook for girls.
    Includes bibliographical references.
    ISBN 1-56887-003-5
    1. Abused children--Mental health. 2. Girls--Family
relationships. 3. Teenage girls--Family relations. 4. Self
-esteem in children. 5. Self-esteem in adolescence. 6. Girls--Life
skills guides. 7. Teenage girls--Life skills guides. 8. Child
psychotherapy. 9. Adolescent psychotherapy. I. Title. II. Title:
You sparkle.
RJ507.A29B47 1994
618.92'858223'008352--dc20
                                  94-15881
                                      CIP

Dedication

This book is dedicated to all of the victimized and neglected children, teenagers, and women whom I have seen in treatment. The courage, endurance, and brilliance they showed in building new lives for themselves has given intense meaning to my life; they brought out my strengths and changed my life forever. This work is also dedicated to my husband Michael, whose respect for my life choices and belief in my abilities has helped me to grow stronger every year.

Acknowledgements

The author would like to thank Dr. Rita Drapkin for reviewing the manuscript to aid its accessibility to children and families with both same and opposite gender sexual orientations, and Ms. Minerva Fyock for her cheerful and untiring aid in manuscript preparation.

Table of Contents

Therapeutic Exercises for Victimized and Neglected Girls:

Applications for Individual, Family, and Group Psychotherapy

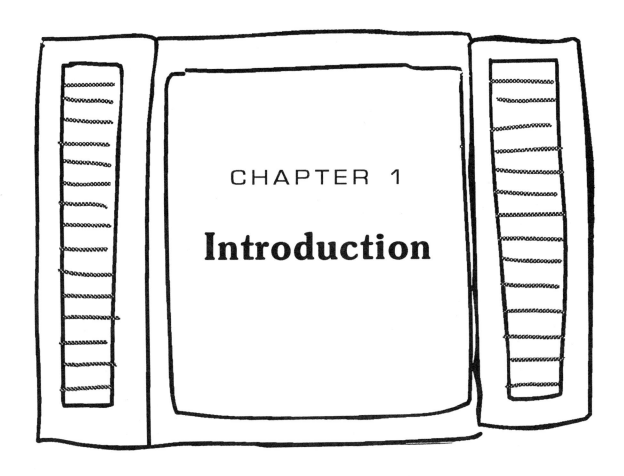

CHAPTER 1

Introduction

Introduction

A national incidence study estimated that, in 1986, more than 1 million children in the United States have been injured as a result of maltreatment and 1/2 million more are estimated to have been at risk for or threatened with maltreatment. Of these maltreated children, 1,100 died as a result of confirmed cases of abuse or neglect (U.S. Department of Health and Human Services, 1988). Neglect is the most prevalent form of maltreatment, followed by physical abuse, emotional abuse, and sexual abuse. Many children are victims of several forms of maltreatment (U.S. Department of Health and Human Services, 1989). These statistics clearly point to the need for treatment services for these populations.

Effective treatment of victimized and/or neglected populations is a challenge. Referrals are often mandated, rather than voluntary, and family and extrafamilial support for treatment is often minimal. These clients are often in a state of constant crisis and have few economic or psychological resources.

This book provides detailed therapeutic exercises for working effectively with these populations. The exercises are not intended to be viewed as an all-inclusive treatment package. Rather, they provide a useful structure from which to introduce difficult topics, teach skills, and depart into more detailed discussions of issues that are highly relevant to victimized and neglected children and their families. The realms covered by the exercises include recognition and identification of feelings, assertive communication and problem solving, constructive peer relationships, constructive parenting, sexuality, physical victimization of children and spouses, and sexual victimization of children. The exercises were designed to be developmentally appropriate for treatment sessions in which the identified client is a school-age or teenage girl. Issues faced by clinicians in providing treatment to these girls are discussed in Chapter 2 (pp. 7-10). The instructions for these exercises, as well as potential problems in successful implementation and possible solutions can be found in Chapter 3 (pp. 11-119).

A major obstacle to providing effective treatment to victimized and neglected girls is that they are often withdrawn prematurely from treatment, losing both an opportunity to "profit maximally" from therapy and the opportunity to experience a healthy termination of their relationship with the therapist and other group members. There are no perfect solutions to this problem. However, one solution is to provide the girls with an alternative means for accessing therapeutic material. The Appendix (pp. A-1 to A-31) presents a handbook for girls that summarizes the information, and reinforces the skill building, covered in the Chapter 3 exercises. Instructions for the use of this handbook are provided.

EXERCISE SELECTION

The therapist needs to use clinical judgment in determining when and if to use an exercise and how to modify it before or during implementation to make it maximally effective for specific girls. It may be appropriate for some girls to go through all the skill-building units contained within Chapter 3 in the order in which they have been presented. For other girls, only some of the skill-building units will be useful and, within units, only some of the exercises will be necessary. As a general guideline, the following skill-building units are considered appropriate for all victimized and neglected girls: identification and expression of feelings, assertive communication, constructive peer relationships, and constructive parenting. The units on sexuality, physical victimization, and sexual victimization are more specialized; a therapist should read the exercise introductions carefully before deciding when and if they are appropriate for a specific girl or girls. In addition, some exercises within a unit may be more or less appropriate depending on the girl's developmental level. For example, within the area of sexuality, the body image exercises may be relevant to the majority of girls, while the exercises aimed at defining the difference between love and lust may be most appropriate for teenagers or younger girls who are actively engaged in consensual sexual activities.

With minor modification of the instructions, it is possible for therapists to introduce the skill-building units in almost any order. Therapists can also decide whether to fully complete units or move back and forth among units. However, in the author's experience, girls need to have mastered the skills learned in two units - identification and expression of feelings and assertive communication - before they profit from the other units. In addition, if victimization issues are focused on too early in the skill-building process, they may generate a stress level so high that girls cannot profit maximally and, moreover, may terminate prematurely from treatment (Berman, 1992).

Each unit consists of several exercises. The order of the exercises within units reflects either the recommended order for presentation or the relative stress level of the material. For example, in the unit on expression and recognition of feelings, Exercise 1 is easier to complete than Exercises 2 and 3. In addition, these last two exercises contain increasingly greater amounts of abuse/neglect-related material, thus requiring greater stress tolerance from the girls.

EXERCISE INSTRUCTIONS

Instructions for using these exercises within individual, family, and group treatment are provided; however, they are not intended to be rigid prescriptions. Within individual and family therapy, the author has used the exercises very selectively and has often modified the instructions. For highly defensive families, structured exercises may be an ideal modality, because it is less threatening to work through exercises than to self-disclose. For other families, structured exercises may be counter-productive, and the therapist may use exercises simply to generate ideas for treatment planning. Group treatment of seriously disturbed girls, due to the larger number of girls and their poor or deviant socialization, can easily become chaotic. Within this modality, the author adheres carefully to the structure of the exercises because it reduces acting out (Berman, 1992). Girls will come from families with many different constellations such as nuclear, single-parent, adoptive, and so on. For simplicity, the exercise directions and handouts are written from the perspective of the nuclear family. The therapist may want to alter the language of the directions and handouts to match the actual constellation of each girl's family.

Chapter 4 (pp. 121-129) describes three case examples to illustrate the use of these exercises in individual, family, and group therapy. These case examples illustrate patterns of behavior that were seen in actual therapy sessions. The names, family configurations, demographic information, and other details have been changed to insure confidentiality.

The Appendix contains the "You Sparkle: A Handbook for Girls." This handbook is designed to be given out to girls at the end of treatment to help reinforce the skill building and summarize the key messages provided during treatment. It will provide the greatest benefit to the girls if it is reviewed with them prior to the termination of treatment. Many girls remain in stressful family circumstances after terminating treatment. They can be encouraged to look through their handbook during times of stress or confusion to gain a sense of support for how they are coping or to gain ideas for how to cope. The handbook can also be sent to a girl who has been withdrawn prematurely from treatment. This may serve to reinforce what she has learned in treatment, provide her with a source of validation for the ideas and values promoted in treatment, and serve as a reminder that the therapist considered her an important person.

CHAPTER 2

Issues for
the Therapists

Issues for
the Therapists

Therapists should expect to face significant challenges to the successful initiation, continuation, and termination of treatment with victimized and neglected girls. Treatment can produce powerful changes; however, despite the best intentions and elegance of techniques, treatment may not progress smoothly or end successfully. Success with these families may need to be defined in terms of more circumscribed goals, such as rendering the home free of violence, rather than the more ambitious goal of making the home an enriching environment for a girl. Sometimes the ambitious goals can be achieved, but oftentimes not.

Multimodal treatment is usually optimal in dealing with the complex problems faced by these populations. However, due to lack of family support for treatment, lack of monetary resources, lack of treatment resources, or transportation difficulties, often only one form of treatment is available. While superficially acknowledging the factors handicapping the accomplishment of ambitious goals, therapists frequently blame themselves, or disengage from these girls, rather than taking a more longsighted view of these girls' treatment needs. Therapists need to maintain close contacts with peers for support and advice to prevent burnout. Peer support becomes especially important when a girl who is much in need of treatment is withdrawn prematurely from all services.

ETHICAL CONCERNS

Therapists working with abused and neglected girls need to constantly monitor levels of dangerousness within the home environment. Insuring the physical safety of the girl is critical and must take precedence over other treatment objectives. The therapist needs to be aware of the power differentials between adults and children within a family. Children may be in increased danger if they are the only family members receiving comprehensive treatment. For example, a violent parent may not appreciate

9

a girl's attempts to communicate openly. Perpetrators of physical or sexual abuse should be involved in family treatment sessions only when other family members want their presence and it is emotionally and physically safe for them to be there (Gruszenski, Brink, & Edleson, 1988). If parents refuse or profit minimally from treatment, and the girl remains with them, therapists are facing limited options. They can clearly spell out for the parents that violent experiences within the home will have an increasingly negative influence on their children. Therapists can also help children develop age-appropriate protection plans. However, it is not realistic to expect children to protect themselves.

The role of Child Protective Services (CPS) in the treatment of these families cannot be overemphasized. Child Protective Services can mandate and maintain families in services, temporarily remove a girl from the home if necessary, and serve as another validating source of reality for the girls. In the author's experience, a therapist working with these girls can expect to call CPS at least once a month to report new abusive incidents. Thus, developing an effective working relationship with CPS is vital. Clients should be told that therapists are mandated by law to report any ongoing abuse before they disclose anything that might lead to such a report.

Finally, if a session has been particularly traumatic for girls, or if they are returning home to a potentially abusive situation, they should be reminded of any 24-hour emergency telephone services that are available. The therapist may need to make follow-up phone calls to girls' homes to verify their safety.

CHAPTER 3

Skill-Building Exercises

Recognition and Identification of Feelings

The following activities help girls identify - and personally experience - a variety of feelings, learn the different reasons that people might have for experiencing these feelings, and learn the different ways that people can respond to these feelings. These exercises are important because many of the girls will have poorly developed or maladaptive social and communication skills. These deficits may be due to neglectful parenting, social isolation, or life experiences that have taught them counterproductive skills such as the denial or suppression of feelings, or that they do not have the "right" to have feelings.

Three skill-building exercises are provided. Each exercise is progressively more difficult, and each involves assignments to act out a word, statement, or scenario. Within each exercise, certain assignments are more stressful or difficult than others. The therapist should decide which assignment, within an exercise, is appropriate for which girl based on her present skill level and ability to tolerate stress. After the basics of an exercise have been mastered, move on to the next one.

Information about feelings that can be emphasized throughout these exercises includes: Everyone has feelings, feelings are never stupid, learning to identify different feelings in yourself and in other people can be hard and takes practice, not everyone feels the same way about things, and it is important to respect other people's feelings even when they are different from yours.

Therapists may face several problems when leading these activities. Some girls may consider the activities "babyish." Others may find them so difficult they become frustrated and give up. One solution to these problems is for the therapist to demonstrate the initial examples. The therapist can model having difficulty with expressing a feeling, feeling embarrassed, or needing helpers. The therapist can also model enjoying and feeling proud for having carried through the exercises and for trying to guess the feelings being acted out by others. The "Feelings List" (p.17) provides a list of feelings to be referred to by the audience. This prevents confusion that could occur if, for example, the audience guessed "angry" while the actors, who were portraying "mad," considered "angry" to be incorrect even though the words are synonymous. The actors should receive a great deal of praise for being persistent and for continuing to try no matter how difficult their assignment.

EXERCISE 1

Recognizing and Expressing Feelings

GOALS

To help girls identify and experience different feelings.

ACTIVITY

1. Girls act out feelings that are written on slips of paper (see "Feeling Word Charades" on p. 18).
2. Whoever is not acting out a feeling serves as the audience and tries to guess the feeling being portrayed. Hand out the "Feelings List" (p.17) to the audience. No one should ever be allowed to give up trying to portray a feeling. If a girl is having difficulty, she is encouraged to ask a member of the audience for help.
3. The girls should act out the feeling until the audience has guessed correctly.
4. If the audience is struggling with the assignment, the therapist can provide clues such as "Does it look like a good or bad feeling?" The therapist may also give suggestions to the actor such as "Use your body posture as well as facial expressions to get the feeling across."

INDIVIDUAL THERAPY INSTRUCTIONS

1. The therapist and the girl take turns acting out feelings. It is recommended that the therapist use a container for the slips of paper that has three sections, one for the easier assignments, one for the moderate assignments, and the third for the difficult assignments. In this way, both the therapist and the girl can anonymously select assignments, yet the therapist can control the difficulty level and stress level of the assignments. As enthusiasm and comfort with the activity builds, the therapist and the girl can challenge each other to draw feelings from the next most difficult section.

FAMILY THERAPY INSTRUCTIONS

1. Family members take turns acting out feelings. The therapist should decide which family member should go first. It is recommended that this be the family member most likely to comply enthusiastically with the assignment.
2. All family members should have a turn before allowing anyone a second turn.
3. Attention should be paid to the developmental level of the client. For example, a basic feeling such as "mad" is most appropriate for a young child.

4. As family members become comfortable with the exercise, the therapist can begin selecting feelings for family members that might help promote insight into their dynamics. For example, a family member who is always angry can try to act out "silly." The individual may continue looking angry - which can help the family realize just how difficult it is for this person to stop being angry. Or, this person may finally have an opportunity to "feel something else" within the context of a family interaction.

5. After everyone has taken at least one turn, teams of family members can then act out a feeling together. The teams can progress from two members to three, and so forth, until the entire family is working together with only the therapist left to serve as the audience.

GROUP THERAPY INSTRUCTIONS

1. Girls take turns acting out the feelings.

    a. The therapist should decide what feeling each girl will be assigned to act out based on the therapist's understanding of the girl's ability to act it out (so it will provide a clear message to the other girls) as well as her readiness to handle the level of stress involved.

    b. After the initial performance anxiety has worn off, the girls may compete with each other to receive the hardest examples to act out. The therapist must insure that this is a constructive rather than a destructive challenge.

    c. If the girls are still profiting from the exercise after everyone has had a turn, the therapist can begin assigning feelings to teams of two, three, and so on.

EXERCISE 1 HANDOUT

Feelings List

I Feel . . .

Happy	Sick	Scared
Proud	Bored	Embarrassed
Comforted	Lonely	Frustrated
Stupid	Mad	Hurt
Curious	Worried	Numb
Silly	Jealous	Tired
Excited	Sad	Rejected
Sorry	Surprised	Hungry

Feeling Word Charades

__Therapist Directions:__ Cut apart the following words and separate by difficulty level.

RELATIVELY EASY	MODERATELY DIFFICULT	DIFFICULT
Happy	Proud	Comforted
Silly	Curious	Stupid
Sick	Excited	Sorry
Mad	Bored	Lonely
Scared	Worried	Jealous
Sad	Surprised	Numb
Tired	Embarrassed	Frustrated
Hungry	Hurt	Rejected

Recognizing How Events Can Influence Feelings

GOAL

Help girls put cause (something happens) together with effect (the feelings that can result).

ACTIVITY

1. The therapist modifies the statements to match the girls' family configurations. For example, "Mom's boyfriend" can be substituted for "Dad."
2. The therapist gives each girl a statement written on a piece of paper (see "Feeling Statement Charades," pp. 21-23).
3. The girl acts out how she would feel if this event involved her. The girl may ask for help in thinking through the assignment.
4. The audience tries to guess the feeling. Hand out "Feelings List" (p. 17) to the audience.
5. Once the correct feeling is guessed, the actor reads the statement aloud and explains why she would have had that feeling.

INDIVIDUAL THERAPY INSTRUCTIONS

1. The therapist and girl take turns responding to the statements. Statements should be selected following the same procedure described in the "Feeling Word Charades."
2. If the girl needs help carrying through the assignment, the therapist and the girl should try to come up with at least two different ways of handling the assignment in order to demonstrate that (a) not everyone would feel the same if that event had happened to them, and (b) not everyone shows the same feeling in the same way.

FAMILY THERAPY INSTRUCTIONS

1. Rewrite the statements to match the clients' family configuration and add adult equivalents. For example, if the child version is "Your parents are laughing," then the adult version is "Your children are laughing."
2. Family members take turns responding to the statements. If family members are having difficulty, they can select anyone that they want to help them think through and act out the assignment (including the therapist).
3. Once the family becomes comfortable with this activity, the therapist can carefully select which family member helps another who is struggling with an assignment. For

example, two alienated siblings might experience a positive moment together if one helped the other successfully carry out an assignment. Similarly, a parent who is inexperienced at helping a child may gain a sense of empowerment from helping the child successfully complete the activity.

GROUP THERAPY INSTRUCTIONS

1. The girls take turns responding to the statements.
2. The girl who is acting out a feeling can request help either in thinking through what to do or in acting it out. Her portrayal should reflect *her* feelings - not how her helpers might feel if the statement referred to them.
3. The therapist needs to monitor the personal reactions of the actors and the audience, because the event described in each statement is likely to have occurred recently in at least one girl's family.

EXERCISE 2 MATERIALS

Feeling Statement Charades

__Therapist Directions:__ Cut apart the following statements and separate by stress level.

LEAST STRESSFUL STATEMENTS

Dad talks to you.	You are alone at lunch time, and you see another girl who is alone.
You invite someone to spend the day with you.	Your parents are laughing.
Your grades in school went up.	You stay home from school.
Someone says they like you.	You go to school.
Mom takes you with her to the store.	You spend time with a friend.
Someone you want to be friends with sits next to you.	You spend time with your brother (or sister).

MODERATELY STRESSFUL STATEMENTS

You go to the doctor.	Someone calls you a liar.
There is no one to talk to.	You forget to do your homework.
You make a mistake at school.	You hit your brother (or sister).
You are alone at home.	Someone at school insults you.
You are alone and then your Mom runs into the room.	A teacher yells at you.
Your sister (or brother) is yelling at you.	There is no one to spend time with.
Your Mom is leaving the house and will not take you with her.	Someone at the park threatens you.

MOST STRESSFUL STATEMENTS

You are sick and your Mom ignores you.	Everyone is yelling.
Dad yells at you.	Your mother is crying.
Dad ignores you.	Mom and Dad are yelling at each other.
Mom and Dad are not talking to each other.	Mom hits you.
Mom yells at you.	Dad hits you.
You are in the hospital.	Your brother (or sister) hits you.

EXERCISE 3

Recognizing and Validating Feelings Caused by Stressful Events

GOALS

To help girls put emotional cause-and-effect relationships together in more complex situations and to discourage denial or minimizing of negative emotions.

ACTIVITY

1. Each girl is given a scenario by the therapist that is written on a piece of paper (see "Feeling Scenario Charades" on pp. 27–28). The girl is to be the main character in the scenario. Members of the audience are selected to help the girl act out the scenario. The remaining audience guesses the content of the scenario.
2. Once the basic content has been correctly identified, the actors express how they would feel if this scenario were really happening to them.
3. All of the least stressful scenarios should be completed before the girls go on to the moderately and then highly stressful scenarios.

INDIVIDUAL THERAPY INSTRUCTIONS

1. The therapist should modify any scenario that requires more than two actors.
2. The therapist and girl work together acting out the scenarios and take turns orchestrating how the scenarios should be portrayed.
3. After acting out a scenario, they should each disclose how they would feel if that scenario had happened to them. The therapist should always validate the feelings expressed by the girl and also bring up alternative feelings that others might have had in the same situation.

FAMILY THERAPY INSTRUCTIONS

1. The therapist needs to use caution and clinical judgment in determining which scenarios to use for a particular family at a particular moment in time. Some of the scenarios might provoke an untherapeutic crisis unless the family has already made considerable progress in treatment. At the right time, some of the scenarios could be used to evoke healing experiences (e.g., if, in the role play of an abusive situation, a previously unsupportive parent is able to provide emotional support to the child). The scenarios can be altered to suit the client's gender and/or family configuration.

2. After acting out a scenario, all family members should be encouraged to express how they would feel if this situation had happened to them and, if appropriate, how they felt watching this situation happen to the actors.

GROUP THERAPY INSTRUCTIONS

1. The girls take turns being given scenarios to act out.
2. The girls in the audience may make judgmental comments about how a given person has reacted to a scenario. The therapist needs to counteract this by underscoring the validity of the many different feelings that may be expressed both by the actors and the audience in response to the scenarios.

EXERCISE 3 MATERIALS

Feeling Scenario Charades

__Therapist Directions:__ Cut apart the following scenarios and separate by difficulty level.

LEAST STRESSFUL SCENARIOS

You are at the park. There is another girl there playing basketball by herself. You would like to play with her, but you don't know her name.

You are sitting in the lunch room at school all by yourself. At the next table there is a whole group of girls laughing and talking. They don't notice you. You try to do something to get their attention.

You are in class at school. The teacher is going down each row asking every student a question about the homework assignment. You did not do the assignment, and it will be your turn soon.

MODERATELY STRESSFUL SCENARIOS

Your mother is about to leave, and you ask her where she is going. She tells you to leave her alone, that she doesn't know where she is going or when she's coming back. You are all alone for hours.

It is 5:00 p.m., and you are having a fight with your brother. Your father comes in and he is really angry. He puts you both in separate corners of the room and tells you to stay there. At 6:00 p.m. Dad has dinner, and at 11:00 p.m. he goes to bed, leaving you both in the corners.

You are having a fight with one of your friends. It starts out as a small fight and ends with you hitting your friend. Your friend runs off crying.

MOST STRESSFUL SCENARIOS

Mom and Dad are having a fight. Dad storms out of the house. Mom asks you to wash the dishes. You shrug your shoulders. She beats you up.

Mom is sitting alone and staring out the window. You come home all excited about your report card. You start to tell your Mom. She screams at you to go away. You try again. She grabs you by the arm and screams, and screams, and screams.

You are alone in the school parking lot. An older boy comes by, begins fondling the private parts of your body, and tries to push you down on the ground. You struggle, but he won't let you go. A friend comes by and helps you. The boy runs away.

You are at a family party, and your uncle wants you to sit on his lap. You don't want to. He keeps pulling on your arm. You finally sit on his lap, but you feel really uncomfortable because he is holding you really tight.

UNIT TWO

Assertive Communication and Problem Solving

The following exercises teach assertive communication and problem-solving skills. These skills are important because many victimized and/or neglected girls behave either passively or aggressively in social and interpersonal situations. Physical and sexual abusers often make their victims feel powerless, unable to control their bodies or their lives. Sexual abusers frequently instruct their victims to lie and act out, or they ignore the protests of their victims. Once the abuse is revealed, the victims may not be believed, increasing the victim's feelings of passivity or their aggressive coping. Neglected girls may feel that only very intense behavior will bring a response or, conversely, that any behavior at all is futile. Aggressive and passive coping may reflect dichotomous thinking - that not being a victim means being a victimizer. Assertiveness provides an alternative to the roles of both victim and victimizer.

Three levels of exercises of increasing difficulty are provided. The first level teaches girls to recognize assertive statements. The second level teaches girls how to reframe nonassertive statements into assertive ones (i.e., to think assertively). The third level helps girls think through how they could assertively handle a situation in which someone was trying to victimize them.

Throughout the assertiveness exercises, the following information should be emphasized: Girls should respect themselves and other people; being assertive does not guarantee a respectful response from others, but assertive behavior is more likely to engender a respectful response from others than aggressive or passive behavior. Detailed discussions of assertive/effective communication can be found in Gorden (1975) and Lange and Jakubowski (1976).

The assertiveness unit is significantly more difficult than the feelings unit. In many ways, the assertiveness exercises encourage behavior that runs counter to how victimized and neglected girls have previously learned to behave or survive. Thus, the girls may become easily frustrated and try to give up. Their frustration may be counteracted by providing additional incentives for achievement. One way to increase incentives is a motivation chart called the "Assertiveness Meter" (see Table 1, p. 31). The meter is shaped like an upside-down thermometer with steps from 1 to 21 going up the shaft and a pic-

29

ture of a rock star (covered with paper tabs) at the bulb end. Appropriate pictures can be found in teen magazines. Each step is labeled, from 1 (Not Assertive), to 21 (Sparklingly Assertive). Girls are told that every three points they earn during an assertiveness exercise moves them up one step on the meter. For every step up the meter, one tab hiding the picture of the rock star is removed and the girls attempt to guess the identity of the rock star. In family sessions, parents and very young children will usually be at a disadvantage in guessing the rock star. It will be up to the therapist in these sessions to promote positive cooperation versus "one-downsmanship" among family members. If the identity of the rock star is guessed before girls reach the last step on the meter, insert a new picture.

TABLE 1: ASSERTIVENESS METER

__Therapist Directions:__ Use this drawing as a guide when developing a motivation chart for your clients. A large drawing of the meter on poster board is recommended. The girls can color one numbered step for every three points they earn.

Picture of a Rock Star covered by small paper tabs should be placed here.	
21	Sparklingly Assertive
20	Rambunctiously Assertive
19	Delightedly Assertive
18	Enthusiastically Assertive
17	Joyfully Assertive
16	Eagerly Assertive
15	Confidently Assertive
14	Cheerfully Assertive
13	Pleasantly Assertive
12	Securely Assertive
11	Modestly Assertive
10	Coolly Assertive
9	Skeptically Assertive
8	Hesitantly Assertive
7	Weakly Assertive
6	Anxiously Assertive
5	Worriedly Assertive
4	Uneasily Assertive
3	Ghostly Assertive
2	Invisibly Assertive
1	Not Assertive

EXERCISE 4

Recognizing Assertive Statements

GOAL

To clarify what an assertive statement is.

ACTIVITY

1. The therapist explains that being assertive means standing up for yourself and expressing your feelings in a way that does not blame, impose on, or try to manipulate other people. Assertive communication includes stating your true feelings about something along with why you feel that way, such as, "I feel mad because you won't share your video games with me." Assertive communication does not contain coercive statements, such as, "If you don't do what I want, I won't care about you"; or "If you don't do this, I won't be able to go back to school." Communicating assertively can be difficult, especially when angry. When passive or aggressive messages have occurred, assertive apologies can be used in attempts to redirect the communication, such as, "I am embarrassed that I tried to force you to change your opinion."

2. After the therapist provides these explanations and demonstrations of assertiveness, each girl receives a copy of "Recognizing Assertive Statements" (p. 35), reads each statement, and decides if they "attack" another person and imply that they have been "bad" or if they are assertive statements that describe a problem between two people and how the speaker feels about it.

3. Girls receive one point for each of the seven statements identified correctly.

4. All points earned are reflected by movement up the assertiveness meter (see Table 1, p. 31).

INDIVIDUAL THERAPY INSTRUCTIONS

1. The therapist explains assertiveness.
2. The therapist reads each statement aloud and the girl attempts to identify it as assertive or blaming.
3. Any misclassified statement should be discussed.

FAMILY THERAPY INSTRUCTIONS

1. The therapist explains assertiveness. Add as many extra examples of assertive versus nonassertive communication as needed to insure that the youngest family members fully understand the concept of assertiveness. Oral examples are preferable to written as the

youngest family members may not be able to read. Having younger children practice making aggressive, passive, and assertive statements can increase their comprehension of the concept. For example, if the parents and the child have a history of conflicts at bedtime, the parent and child could be coached through three types of interactions. In the first type, both the parent and the child can respond passively. In the second type, both the parent and the child can be assertive, and so on. (*Assertive Example:* Parent - "I know you want to stay up, but I want you to go to bed because I am concerned about your getting enough sleep." Child - "I feel mad because you want me to go to bed, and I want to watch TV.") For the full assertive effect, both the parent and the child would have to make these statements in a self-confident rather than a whiny or aggressive tone of voice. The family should not attempt to solve the bedtime conflict yet. This exercise is just a first step in beginning assertive problem solving by developing an understanding of what assertive communication is and is not.

2. After assertiveness has been clearly defined, the therapist can decide whether it will be more effective for a given family to work as a unit in recognizing assertive statements or if a team approach would be more appropriate (parent team versus child team, or parent-child dyads, etc.).

3. Each team can earn points for correct identification of the statements; points are combined for movement up the assertiveness meter. When the assertiveness meter does not seem appropriate for a family, another incentive system can be negotiated. For example, a point system could be instituted in which children earn privileges based on the number of assertiveness points they have achieved.

GROUP THERAPY INSTRUCTIONS

1. The therapist defines assertiveness.
2. The group should be divided into teams of three or four people. Each team gets a copy of the statements and attempts to recognize which ones are assertive.
3. Each team receives one point for each of the seven statements that they identify correctly.
4. The points earned by all teams are added together in moving up the assertiveness meter.

EXERCISE 4 HANDOUT

Recognizing Assertive Statements

__Directions:__ Put a "B" in the blank if the statement blames another person; put an "A" in the blank if the statement demonstrates assertive behavior.

_____ 1. You know you're not supposed to get into the refrigerator without asking. You are just trying to annoy me!

_____ 2. I feel frustrated that you never do your homework like I have asked you to.

_____ 3. Why are you so mean to me? You don't love me!

_____ 4. I was very worried when you didn't come home when you were supposed to. I was scared to death that something had happened to you!

_____ 5. I'm trying to talk to the class, and I really get frustrated when you're talking to your neighbor.

_____ 6. You little flirt!

_____ 7. I'm feeling pretty grouchy because I think I just flunked a test.

EXERCISE 5

Making Assertive Statements

GOAL

To practice "thinking" assertively.

ACTIVITY

1. The therapist gives a copy of "Making Assertive Statements" (pp. 39-40) to each girl. Girls rewrite the statements into an assertive form. The therapist helps the girls think through how the person making the statement might feel and what the person's problem might be.
2. Therapists issue 0, 1/2, or 1 point for each rewritten statement depending on how well it reflects assertive behavior.
3. All the points earned are reflected by movement up the assertiveness meter (see Table 1, p. 31).
4. The therapist needs to engender an atmosphere of fun and challenge or this exercise may seem like a test to the girls. For example, the therapist should not insist that girls come up with "perfect" revisions for each statement. Assertive communication will be difficult for these girls. The therapist needs to insure that even if progress is slow, there is a sense of steady progress. If the atmosphere becomes tense, the therapist can give an inane but assertive statement in response to an item.

INDIVIDUAL THERAPY INSTRUCTIONS

1. It may be unnecessary or too demanding to go through all 20 statements with one girl. The therapist should select the statements to work on that may be most appropriate for the girl.
2. The therapist brainstorms with the girl potential problems and feelings expressed within the statements.
3. If, while brainstorming, the therapist rewrites a statement, the girl should be encouraged to create another transformation of the statement or take the lead in analyzing the next statement.

FAMILY THERAPY INSTRUCTIONS

1. The therapist should replace some of the statements with parental equivalents. For example, if the child statement is "You are a terrible mother," then the parent statement should be "You are a terrible child."

2. The therapist should decide if the family unit should discuss and respond to each item, if there should be teams (e.g., parent versus child dyads or parent-child dyads), or if individuals should respond to items. Selectively assigning particular statements to certain family members may foster mutual insight (e.g., if parents rewrite "child" statements and children rewrite "adult" statements). Teamwork, on the other hand, provides the opportunity for practicing constructive family relationships. For example, in families where positive, nuturant parent-child interactions have been minimal, an effective parent-child team experience may serve as a beginning step to a new and more constructive relationship. The therapist must monitor team interactions and intervene with humor or other tactics if interactions are not constructive.

3. The incentives instituted in the Family Therapy Instructions for Exercise 4 (p. 34) can be continued if appropriate.

GROUP THERAPY INSTRUCTIONS

1. Divide the group into teams of three or four people making each team responsible for rewriting as many statements as they can in 20 minutes.
2. The group then reconvenes to hear each team's rewritten statements and to give each team points for how assertive the rewrites are.
3. The differences between the teams' rewritten statements can be used to emphasize that there is no "right" or "perfect" way to express a thought assertively.
4. The therapist should liberally praise all efforts.
5. All the points earned by both teams result in movement up the meter.

EXERCISE 5 HANDOUT

Making Assertive Statements

Directions: *Rewrite each statement to be an assertive statement.*

Tips: If the statement is "You are mean," the assertive statement might be "I *feel* hurt *because* you hit me" or "I *want* you to stop hitting me *because* it hurts."

1. You're so spoiled! You get whatever you want from Mom, and I get nothing.

2. Leave me alone - you never do what I want.

3. What business is it of yours? You never help me.

4. Do what I want, or you're not my friend.

5. I'll help you with your schoolwork if you will go out with me.

6. You're a witch - you never let me spend time with my friends.

7. Nothing is the matter. Leave me alone or I'll get into more trouble.

8. I can't stop singing; just ignore me.

9. I'm not mad; just stay away from me *forever*!

10. If you'll be friends with me, I'll do anything you want.

11. You're stealing all of my friends.

12. I don't have any problems - everyone is just unfair.

13. Stop nagging me or I'll never come back.

14. How dare you lie about me.

15. Please take me with you, please, please, please!

16. Go ahead and study - you think you're so smart.

17. If you cared about me you would do my homework.

18. Go ahead - try and kill me; you can't hurt me.

19. You're a terrible mother.

20. I'm only your sister; you'll never spend time with me - only with your friends.

EXERCISE 6

Responding Assertively to Problems

GOALS

To help girls identify problems, how they feel about them, and how to think through assertive solutions to them.

ACTIVITY

1. A girl is given a scenario to act out by the therapist (see "Responding Assertively to Problem Scenarios" on p. 43). The therapist should consider the age and skill level of the girls in choosing which scenario to assign to them. A girl may ask other girls or the therapist to help act out the scenario if needed.
2. After the scenario has been acted out, the therapist asks what happened and how the people in the scenario were feeling.
3. The therapist then asks the girls to demonstrate an assertive way to solve the problem described in the scenario.
4. Girls are given points for their performance in both phases of the exercise that are applied to movement up the assertion meter (see Table 1, p. 31).

INDIVIDUAL THERAPY INSTRUCTIONS

1. First, the therapist and the girl work together on each scenario. They take turns orchestrating how the scenario will be acted out. After acting out a scenario, they reveal how they felt within their role. They then discuss at least two assertive responses the characters could have made to resolve the problem. They can act out one or more of these assertive responses to "try them on for size."
2. The therapist should emphasize that there is no "perfect" way to respond assertively to an interpersonal problem and that responding assertively does not guarantee a happy ending.

FAMILY THERAPY INSTRUCTIONS

1. The therapist needs to carefully review the scenarios to determine if they are appropriate for a given family. For example, is it safe for a family to work through a scenario involving child abuse? The therapist can modify the scenarios to suit the needs of a

particular family. For example, if a major source of conflict within the family is two siblings fighting over possessions, then some of the existing scenarios may be altered to parallel (but not exactly match) these conflicts or create new scenarios to fulfill this function.

2. The therapist should take into account the developmental level of the family members to determine who should be put in charge of acting out which scenarios.

3. After a scenario has been acted out, the first step is to define what happened and how people felt while clarifying appropriate parent-child boundaries. The therapist asks what happened, who is involved in the event, who should be involved, and how each participant is feeling.

4. Next, the actors are to demonstrate an assertive response to the problem portrayed in the scenario. To reinforce boundaries, clients should discuss who should be involved in the solution and what they would like to happen in the future.

5. After following these instructions for several scenarios, the family may be ready to use assertive communication to discuss a current family issue without the use of scenarios.

6. The incentives instituted in the Family Therapy Instructions for Exercise 4 (p. 34) can be continued if appropriate.

GROUP THERAPY INSTRUCTIONS

1. The therapist should use care in determining which girl is put in charge of which scenario, because each scenario is likely to "hit home" for at least one girl.

2. The therapist asks members of the audience (not any of the girls who took part in the acting) to demonstrate an assertive response to the problem described in the scenario. It is important for those girls who were not chosen as helpers to have a vital role in the activity; otherwise, they will feel rejected and may stop paying attention to or disrupt the activity.

EXERCISE 6 MATERIALS

Responding Assertively
to Problem Scenarios

Therapist Directions: **Cut apart**
the following scenarios and hand out separately.

You have just come home from school, and you have promised a friend you will go to the store with her. Your mother insists that you stay home and wash dishes.

You are with a group of three girls. You would really like to play basketball but, as usual, everyone else wants to play kickball.

Your father told your sister to rake the back yard. Your sister ran out the door, so your father made you do it. Your sister has now come home.

You are the only friend that Sarah has; you have spent the day at school talking and joking with Amy. At the end of the day, Sarah walks by you and calls you a bitch.

You have just begun cutting the grass. Your father is inside watching TV. A friend comes by and invites you to the beach. Her family will be leaving in 10 minutes.

Last night your mom and dad had a big fight. You were so sad and scared that you forgot to do your homework. Your teacher yelled at you and called you lazy in front of the whole class.

You borrowed your mother's earrings without asking. She sees you with them on and starts yelling at you.

You and your date go to the movies. Your date wants you to take your clothes off. You really like this person, but you don't want to take your clothes off.

UNIT THREE

Peer Relationships

These exercises provide information about how to recognize and build constructive relationships with peers with an emphasis on how to avoid exploiting or being exploited by peers. Peer relationships become increasingly important to girls as they progress from early childhood through late adolescence. Due to past social isolation and possible media disclosure of abuse, victimized and neglected girls may have difficulty forming and maintaining good relationships with peers. Neglected girls may have been stigmatized by peers because of their poor personal hygiene or lack of clean clothing. Sexually victimized girls may have increased difficulty relating constructively to peers. They may use the "skills" their abusers taught them to try to attract friends, and, due to their sexualized development and the public's knowledge of their abuse, they may be sexual targets for maladjusted peers.

Four exercises are provided. The first two deal with the recognition of the qualities and behaviors involved in a constructive friendship. The second two deal with defining and constructively developing a romantic relationship.

Important themes to highlight throughout the exercises are that people should strive to be good friends to others and avoid exploiting or being exploited by peers. The focus is on *striving* to be a good friend, because no one is perfect and behaves constructively at all times. Girls need to practice being responsive to the needs of other people and responding assertively to relationship problems. This is presented as a three-step process. For example, if someone a girl really likes is doing destructive things, then the first step is for the girl to assess whether it is physically safe to try to talk through the problem (dangerousness assessment). If the relationship problem does not involve violence (or other dangerous behavior), then the second step is for the girl to talk assertively to the person about the problem and try to have a reciprocal discussion of both people's thoughts and feelings. If this discussion is successful, the third step is to try to find a solution to the problem that both people can respect. However, if after Step 2 the "friend" continues to not respect the girl's body or feelings, then the girl needs to get help from all of her constructive friends to stay away from this destructive person.

Obstacles to these activities are poor reading or writing skills. Therapists need to assess the literacy level of the girls and modify the assignments to prevent counterproductive frustration.

EXERCISE 7

Defining Good and Bad Friends

GOAL

To help girls define constructive friendships.

ACTIVITY

1. The girls are given sheets of blank paper and asked to create a list of answers to the question "What is a friend?" The therapist insures that the list contains three themes: someone who likes them, someone with whom the girls are comfortable talking, and someone who is fun to be with.
2. Second, the therapist brings up the issue of constructive friendships (i.e., there are good and bad friends). Both good and bad friends try to be helpful, but the bad friend just gets you into more trouble.
3. The girls are then asked to generate lists of good and bad friend characteristics. Table 2 (pp. 49-50) contains a sample list of issues to help guide the therapist during the activity.

INDIVIDUAL THERAPY INSTRUCTIONS

1. The therapist and girl work together to define friendship.
2. The therapist can encourage the girl to use her ongoing relationships with peers and with the therapist as sources of ideas for the good and bad friend lists.

FAMILY THERAPY INSTRUCTIONS

1. The family works together to define friendship.
2. Family members may have few if any constructive peer relationships and thus struggle in their attempts to discriminate "good" from "bad" friend behaviors. All sincere suggestions made by family members need to be treated with respect. However, the therapist may need to expand or rework these examples to insure that they fit constructively into the activity.
3. Family members may realize, or come to realize during the exercise, that they are not involved in any constructive relationships. After validating this, a therapist needs to engender hope that the family can develop a positive social network.

GROUP THERAPY INSTRUCTIONS

1. The group works together to define friendship.

2. The therapist separates the group into two teams to generate lists of the characteristics of good and bad friends.

3. Once these tasks are accomplished, the teams can be brought together for a comparison and discussion of their work.

4. In completing this activity, girls may discover that they are socially isolated or involved in highly negative peer relationships. The relationships that they are building in group can be used as examples of constructive friendships that can be replicated outside the therapy setting.

TABLE 2: SAMPLE QUALITIES
OF GOOD AND BAD FRIENDS

QUALITIES OF GOOD FRIENDS

1. Good friends really care about you and will:

   a. listen to your feelings and will not make fun of them.
   b. never intentionally hurt you even if they hurt you accidentally.
   c. be considerate of what you like and don't like and will compromise with you.

2. Good friends encourage you to do constructive things (things that are good for you) and:

   a. help you if you are in trouble even if they are busy or mad at you.
   b. encourage you to face your problems no matter how scary the problems are.
   c. tell you the truth and help you tell the truth.
   d. talk to you after fighting with you and remain your friend.
   e. keep your secrets except to tell someone who will help you.

QUALITIES OF BAD FRIENDS

1. Bad friends don't really care about you and:

   a. hurt your feelings intentionally.
   b. say mean things about you behind your back but may be nice to you when you meet face to face.
   c. lie about you.
   d. tell your secrets when they are mad at you.

2. Bad friends take advantage of you and:

   a. break a rule and let you take the blame.
   b. abuse your body.
   c. threaten not to be your friend if you don't do what *they* want.
   d. borrow your things without asking or won't return your things when you ask them to.
   e. lie to you or encourage you to lie to keep out of trouble.

49

f. say nice things to you just to get you to do their homework or give them your money.

3. Bad friends encourage you to be self-destructive by doing things which cause you harm and:

   a. encourage you to cut class because you don't like the teacher.
   b. encourage you to drink alcohol or take drugs when you are lonely or sad.
   c. suggest that you run away from home when you are fighting with your parents.
   d. suggest you steal something when you want it but have no money to buy it.
   e. encourage you to be mean to someone else when you feel sad or mad.

EXERCISE 8

Recognizing Constructive Friendship Behavior

GOALS

To illustrate constructive help from a friend and to help girls begin to develop constructive friendship skills.

ACTIVITY

1. The girl is given a scenario to act out (see "Friendship Scenarios" on pp. 53-54).
2. The girl can ask for help from others.
3. After the scenario has been acted out, the audience discusses the following questions:

   a. How is this helping the person?
   b. Is this a good friend or bad friend?
   c. What alternate solutions are there to this problem?

INDIVIDUAL THERAPY INSTRUCTIONS

1. The therapist and the girl take turns reading the scenarios aloud.
2. For each scenario, they discuss the questions raised in the activity description. The therapist should not expect the girl to use sound judgment in evaluating the early scenarios. For example, the girl may say that a scenario that is meant to reflect bad-friend behavior represents good-friend behavior. In such a case, in the final discussion of the scenario, the therapist can insure that the alternative solutions generated contain examples of good-friend behavior. Insight and skill building are expected to occur over the course of completing the entire exercise.

FAMILY THERAPY INSTRUCTIONS

1. The therapist should review the scenarios and modify them in terms of gender and activity to make them appropriate for the family constellation.
2. Family members take turns acting out scenarios. The therapist should take into account the developmental level of the family members in determining who should be put in charge of acting out which scenarios.
3. The therapist should carefully assess the friendship/social skills of the parents and attempt to empower them to help their children discuss the scenarios.

51

4. After the family has established a pattern of constructively and successfully dealing with the scenarios, they can begin to practice working through any peer relationship problems that are confronting their family.

GROUP THERAPY INSTRUCTIONS

1. Group members should take turns acting out the scenarios.
2. The audience should discuss the three questions raised in the activity description. Girls can be expected to disagree over what represents good and bad friend behavior. The therapist needs initially to support all sides; however, over the course of all the scenarios, the therapist should help the girls develop criteria for assessing constructive versus destructive help.

EXERCISE 8 MATERIALS

Friendship Scenarios

__Therapist Directions:__ Cut apart the following scenarios and hand out.

You have two close friends named Amy and Sue. Amy invites you to go to the movies. Sue calls you and invites you out for the same day. You tell her you are sick and have to stay in bed.

You've just had a fight with your mom, and you have run over to a friend's house. Your friend listens to you talk about how you feel. She then helps you figure out what to say to your mom when you go home and walks back to your house with you as moral support.

There is a really cute person in class and you want this person to become interested in you. You are not really sure what to do. You ask a friend for advice. Your friend suggests that you unbutton the first three buttons on your shirt and lean over while asking the person a question.

You were beaten up by your mother. You tell your friend the next day at school. Your friend tells you to go and tell the counselor at school. She walks down to the office with you.

You are at a slumber party with about six other girlfriends. They all decide to play a game that you don't want to play. Your friend whispers in your ear, "This is boring. Let's go off and listen to records."

You think that your English teacher hates you and you feel that he is always picking on you in class. Your friend sees you crying and wants to cheer you up. She says, "I've got $3. Let's cut English class, and I'll treat you to fries at McDonalds."

You and a friend have had a big fight. You call each other nasty names and scream a lot. Another friend comes up to you later, and you tell her about the fight. She says, "I would have punched her if she had called me half the names she called you. I heard that she cheated on a test last week."

53

You are in a store with a friend. You really want some new makeup, but you don't have the money to buy it. The saleswoman has been nasty to both of you. Your friend says, "You take the makeup, I'll watch out for the saleswoman. She's a witch - it will serve her right."

You don't understand the math homework assignment that is due tomorrow. Your friend had no trouble completing it. Your friend says she would be glad to come over tonight and help you practice with the examples in the book so that you will be able to figure out the homework on your own.

You are on a date. The other person is pressuring you to have sex. You do not know if you should or not. This person says, "If you love me, you will have sex with me. I am going to leave you if you don't."

EXERCISE 9

Defining Good and Bad Romantic Relationships

GOAL

To begin defining a healthy romantic relationship.

ACTIVITY

1. A discussion of what the girls find appealing and unappealing in someone they would date is initiated. The therapist should draw parallels during this discussion between what makes a good friend and what makes someone a good date.
2. The girls are given sheets of blank paper and asked to generate lists of the characteristics of good and bad dates and then discuss why each item belongs on each list.
3. The therapist should provide suggestions and samples as appropriate. Table 3 (p.57) contains sample good and bad date qualities to help guide the therapist.
4. The therapist should be sensitive to the possibility that some girls may be experiencing same-gender as well as, or instead of, opposite-gender sexual interests.

INDIVIDUAL THERAPY INSTRUCTIONS

1. The therapist and girl take turns coming up with examples of what they find appealing and unappealing in a date to put into good and bad characteristics lists.
2. After creating these lists, the therapist and girl reanalyze each list to determine if each example is on the appropriate list. To make this critique less threatening, the therapist can intentionally suggest an item that, during the critique, they both decide is not appropriate for the "good" list. For example, the therapist can initially suggest that "A good date is mysterious," citing that a mysterious person is exciting to be with. Later, the therapist could question this "good" placement by suggesting that people could be mysterious because (a) they are hiding things from you, (b) they don't feel comfortable sharing with you, and/or (c) they are lying to you.

FAMILY THERAPY INSTRUCTIONS

1. The therapist needs to be sensitive to the sexual orientation and experiences of family members. This exercise may not be appropriate in a family format for children who have been sexually abused by a same-gender abuser and/or if the child gives indications of having same-gender sexual interests. Homophobia is very common within American families. Thus, the therapist should expect that any discussion of same-gender dating interests within a family session may lead to an explosive rather than a

constructive discussion. Discussions of same-gender dating may need to be carried out within individual sessions with a child unless the family has made very significant progress on earlier communication and assertiveness exercises and the family's rapport with the therapist is very strong. In most cases of a same-gender orientation, this exercise might best be delayed until the family has successfully dealt with the sexuality and/or sexual victimization exercises.

2. Unless parents have engaged in at least one constructive romantic relationship, they may be poor role models for their children in the romantic sphere. In this situation, the therapist may want to practice this activity with the parents alone before including the children to insure that the parents will provide constructive help to their children during the exercise.

GROUP THERAPY INSTRUCTIONS

1. The girls should discuss attractive and unattractive dates as a group.
2. Following this, the group forms two teams to create the good and bad date lists.
3. After these lists are completed, the whole group can generate master lists and discuss the similarities and differences between the lists.
4. As homophobia is common in American society, the therapist can expect the girls to make prejudicial statements about a same-gender sexual orientation if this issue is raised. The therapist can respond to these statements matter-of-factly and model nonjudgmental behavior. If the therapist knows or suspects that any of the girls have same-gender sexual interests, these should be discussed in individual sessions to prevent the group from scapegoating this individual.

TABLE 3: SAMPLE QUALITIES OF GOOD AND BAD DATES

QUALITIES OF GOOD DATES

1. A good date is someone who:

    a. likes you exactly the way you are.
    b. respects your thoughts and feelings.
    c. is always honest with you.
    d. cares about you when you are sick.
    e. cares about what you like to do.
    f. wouldn't drink alcohol or take drugs.
    g. wouldn't hit you.
    h. would be polite to your family and friends.

QUALITIES OF BAD DATES

1. A bad date is someone who:

    a. might lie to you.
    b. might scare you or hit you.
    c. might make fun of your thoughts or feelings.
    d. might try to force you to do things you don't want to do.
    e. might steal, drink, or take drugs.
    f. might be rude to your family and friends.
    g. might encourage you to skip school or neglect your homework.

EXERCISE 10

Developing Constructive Romantic Relationships

GOAL

To generate strategies for developing constructive romantic relationships.

ACTIVITY

1. The girls are given sheets of blank paper and asked to create lists of constructive and destructive strategies in response to the questions:

   a. Where do you begin?
   b. What should you do?

   Due to developmental level, or a past history of destructive relationships, girls may need significant help discriminating between constructive and destructive strategies.

2. The therapist can use the sample provided in Table 4 (p. 61) for ideas about "Do's" and "Don'ts."

3. The girls in treatment may range from being obsessed with their sexual feelings to being unaware of having any sexual feelings. Thus, after a general discussion of dating, the therapist needs to decide if it is most appropriate to go on to another unit or discuss other topics related to dating. Other issues that could be discussed include explicit and implicit family messages about sexuality and how to handle wanted and unwanted sexual overtures from peers.

INDIVIDUAL THERAPY INSTRUCTIONS

1. If the girl is not interested in dating, this activity may be inappropriate.
2. If the girl is interested in dating, but has no romantic relationship at this time, follow through with the basic activity.
3. If the girl has a specific romantic interest, the therapist should assess the situation for safety. This is particularly important if the girl is a sexual abuse victim or a witness of parental violence. If the romantic interest is "safe" and age-appropriate, the therapist should facilitate a discussion of how the girl could maintain or try to initiate a constructive relationship with this person. If the romantic interest may be a danger to the girl, the treatment session needs to focus on these safety concerns.

FAMILY THERAPY INSTRUCTIONS

1. The therapist needs to evaluate whether to start this exercise with or without the children being present. If the parents are involved in a destructive relationship and/or used destructive strategies while they were dating, then parent-only sessions are needed. Children can be included once the parents have a basic commitment to the ideas expressed in Tables 3 and 4 (pp. 57 and 61).
2. The exercise will be most effective for the children if their parents can be empowered to take a leadership role in carrying it through.

GROUP THERAPY INSTRUCTIONS

1. The girls can be divided into small groups based on their level of interest in dating. Each group can proceed with the activity at the level of detail that is appropriate to their interests.
2. Following these discussions, the group can be re-formed and the lists of strategies shared. This provides all the girls with a more comprehensive perspective.
3. As the lists are shared, the therapist should emphasize that:

   a. not all girls are interested in or begin dating at the same time.
   b. as girls get older, they are more likely to be interested in dating, and romantic interests may seem more important to them than regular friendship.
   c. it is more important to have constructive friendships than to have romantic friendships *per se*.
   d. girls who are not dating are not rejects; they just aren't dating yet.

TABLE 4: DO'S AND DON'TS FOR DEVELOPING A CONSTRUCTIVE ROMANTIC RELATIONSHIP

DO BE ASSERTIVE AND BE YOURSELF BY:

1. smiling.
2. talking about something you have in common, such as school, homework, and movies.
3. acting like you normally do.
4. wearing clean clothes.
5. practicing good grooming.

DON'T ABUSE YOURSELF OR LET OTHERS TAKE ADVANTAGE OF YOU BY:

1. putting yourself down to make them feel good.
2. acting sexy by walking in a slinky way, wearing clothes that are too tight or revealing, wearing too much makeup, or talking like you have a lot of sexual experience.
3. lying about your age or about your life to seem cool.
4. smoking, drinking, or taking drugs.
5. saying insulting "smart" comments to get their attention.

UNIT FOUR

Parental Relationships

These exercises provide information about family roles, boundaries, and responsibilities. These exercises are important because many adults have children without considering if they can or want to take on the responsibilities and challenges of parenthood. Once they are parents, they may lack the knowledge of child development, the skills in parenting, or the willingness to make the personal sacrifices that may be needed to raise a family without violence or neglect. As a result, children of unprepared parents may receive erratic, poor quality, or abusive parenting. Girls need to understand that parents are responsible for the physical, emotional, and developmental needs of children, and they need to be able to discriminate healthy from destructive parenting practices.

There are three exercises in this unit. In the first exercise, healthy versus problematical parental behaviors are discussed. The value of parental nurturance in socializing children is highlighted. In the second exercise, contracting is illustrated as a mechanism for clarifying implicit parental and child responsibilities and freedoms within the family and engendering respect for the parental role. In the third exercise, alternative parenting situations are explored and their role in providing for the needs of children is highlighted.

Adult-child boundaries need to be clarified throughout the exercises. Other important themes that can be raised include the following: The parent role is difficult and deserves respect; all parents make mistakes; when parents need help they should turn to other adults; seeking help is a sign of strength, not weakness; if a parent or parents are unable or unwilling to take proper care of children, it is the responsibility of other adults to take on these responsibilities; the benefits of child rearing - gaining a sense of personal accomplishment and reciprocal nurturance - can balance out the difficulties and sacrifices inherent in child rearing.

Research has pointed out the links between healthy nurturance and inhibition of aggression with the development of prosocial behavior in children (Eron, 1987; Garbarino, Kostelny, & Dubrow, 1991; Koesnter, Weinberger, & Franz, 1990). However, a major obstacle to the successful implementation of the parenting exercises is that parents may view nurturance as unnecessary or counterproductive to effective child rearing. In the author's experience, it is difficult for adults who have received minimal nurturance themselves to understand or be able to provide nurturance to others. These difficul-

63

ties may be overcome by focusing first on the parents' needs. Through demonstrations of respect and support for the difficulties of parenting, and underscoring the parents' own childhood and adulthood "right to nurturance," the clinician can model and provide nurturance to the parents; the parents may then be more receptive to providing nurturance to their own children.

EXERCISE 11

Analyzing Parenting Behavior

GOALS

To help girls recognize inappropriate parenting practices and identify examples of healthy physical or emotional nurturance.

ACTIVITY

1. The girls analyze the parenting behavior illustrated in each of six "Parenting Scenarios" (see pp. 67-68). The therapist can facilitate each analysis by asking the following questions:

   a. What is the problem?
   b. How are the parents trying to solve it?
   c. Is there another way?

2. Important themes for the therapist to repeat throughout the exercises include:

   a. good parenting includes age-appropriate physical and emotional nurturance.
   b. bad parenting includes children consistently taking care of themselves or their parents (Neglect) or children being victimized (Sexual or Physical Abuse).
   c. quality nurturance is time-consuming but benefits parents by bringing meaning to their lives, increasing their feelings of self-worth, and bringing them nurturance from their children (Erikson, 1963).

INDIVIDUAL THERAPY INSTRUCTIONS

1. The therapist and girl take turns reading the scenarios aloud and asking each other questions about them.
2. Afterward, they can discuss the level of physical and emotional nurturance the girl is currently receiving from her parents. If the nurturance is inadequate, the child can be encouraged to seek appropriate nurturance from other adults. The theme that, although children need nurturance, they don't have to receive it from their parents, can be stressed.

FAMILY THERAPY INSTRUCTIONS

1. The therapist needs to assess whether a family is ready to work together on the scenarios or if sessions with the involved parent or the parental dyad are necessary first.

2. After analyzing all of the scenarios, the family can discuss the nurturance currently available within their family. Family members can be encouraged to request additional nurturance if appropriate. The therapist must insure that any additional contracts for nurturance are age-appropriate.

3. Additional adult-only sessions with the therapist may be appropriate to discuss alternative forms of child guidance.

   a. *Parent Effectiveness Training* (Gordon, 1975) is a helpful resource for parents.
   b. *Parent Education for Low Income Families with Young Children* (M. Mischley, L. Mischley, & Ingold, 1983) is a helpful resource for therapists and it contains many handouts and guidelines for parent training.

GROUP THERAPY INSTRUCTIONS

1. Each girl takes a turn reading a scenario aloud and leading the discussion of it.
2. Afterward, the therapist expands the discussion to the quality of nurturance available within the girls' current home situation. If the level of nurturance is inadequate, the girls can discuss whether it would be safe and/or productive to assertively request more nurturance. The therapist should stress that, while the girls need nurturance, they do not have to receive all of it from their parents.

EXERCISE 11 HANDOUT

Parenting Scenarios

<u>Directions:</u> Read each scenario and then try to answer these questions: What's the problem? How are people trying to solve it? Is there another way?

1. Diane is 12 years old. She is living with her father in the country. She has become increasingly sick over the past few weeks. When she coughs, fluid comes up. She has a high fever and her nose is running. Yesterday, a school counselor called her father and recommended that Diane be taken to a physician. Today, Dad has left her at home with some over-the-counter remedies and told her to contact a physician if she feels like it.

2. Karen is 14 years old. She has come home from school crying. As she entered the house she slammed the door. Crying and swearing, she stomped up the stairs to the second floor. She slammed her bedroom door and then turned on some rock music full blast. Her mother was coming out of the kitchen as Karen came in. When she saw that Karen was crying, she turned around and went back into the kitchen. She thought to herself, "Least said, soonest mended."

3. Cynthia is 17 years old. She has a history of petty thievery. She has been accused of stealing $50 from a teacher's wallet. Her parents go with her to the principal's office and scream at him for falsely accusing their daughter. They threaten to withdraw Cynthia from school if the matter is pursued.

4. Lisa is 12 years old. She told her mother that she had been sexually assaulted by the boy who lives across the street. This boy is the son of the mother's only friend. Mother insists that this boy could not have done this. Lisa begins to shout and then to scream at her mother. Mother begins to walk away in disgust. Lisa grabs her mother's arm. Mother turns around and shoves Lisa into the wall and slaps her face.

5. Martha is 14 years old. She spends the day with her father shopping and going to the movies. They have a great time. When they get home her mother has gone out. Martha thanks her dad for the nice day. He pulls her into his arms. He says she should come to his room so he can show her how much he loves her.

6. Diane is 10 years old. She has been suspended from school for swearing at the math teacher. This is her third suspension in the past month. Diane's mother has locked her in the basement. Mom said that Diane would have to remain in the basement until she learned self-control.

EXERCISE 12

Making Family Contracts

GOALS

To engender respect for the many implicit responsibilities of adults within a family and to illustrate how an individual's freedom to make decisions within a family must be balanced with responsibilities if family members are to receive appropriate care.

ACTIVITY

1. The "Freedoms and Responsibilities Contract" (see p. 71) is used to illustrate how contracting can be used to negotiate changes in how family members get their needs met. The contract consists of freedoms a teenage girl wants and the responsibilities to parallel these freedoms that her parents negotiate with her to insure that her physical, emotional, and developmental needs are adequately met.

2. Information to underscore in discussing the contract include the following points:

   a. Parents have the final responsibility for the physical, emotional, and developmental caretaking of their children.

   b. Greater life control also entails greater life responsibilities; otherwise, someone is being abused or neglected.

   c. Healthy family life does not require perfection from family members; however, the abuse and neglect of children or parents are never acceptable.

INDIVIDUAL THERAPY INSTRUCTIONS

1. The therapist and girl review and discuss the contract example. The therapist then helps the girl develop a contract she wishes existed in her family.

   a. While developing this contract, the therapist initiates discussions of the exercise themes.

   b. If appropriate, the therapist encourages the client to discuss this contract with her caretakers.

FAMILY THERAPY INSTRUCTIONS

1. The therapist hands out a copy of the contract to each family member and initiates a discussion of it.

2. The family negotiates a contract that they would like to exist within their family. This may take several sessions to complete. The therapist initiates discussions of the exercise themes during negotiation of the contract and tries to develop mutual empathy among family members. After the contract is completed, family members sign it, indicating their intention to fulfill their promised obligations irrespective of the behavior of other family members. The therapist should monitor the level of success of contract implementation over time and praise family members who are following through with their part of the contract. The signatures can be used to remind people of their commitment to honor the contract.

GROUP THERAPY INSTRUCTIONS

1. The therapist hands out a copy of the contract to each girl and then initiates a discussion of it.
2. The group is divided into teams of three or four people, and each team develops a contract they wish existed in their families.
3. The group reunites to share the contracts and discuss what they like and dislike about each other's contracts. The therapist underscores the difficulties inherent in parenting.

EXERCISE 12 HANDOUT

Freedoms and Responsibilities Contract

FREEDOMS WANTED BY TEEN	RESPONSIBILITIES ACCEPTED BY TEEN
Greater independence in planning my life including the freedom to have more control over:	To meet my own physical and emotional health and safety needs without jeopardizing the needs of other family members, I will:
1. Scheduling my meals	1A. Notify my parents 2 hours in advance if I want to share a family meal.
	1B. Use care in making my own meals so that food intended for a family meal is not eaten.
2. Scheduling my social activities	2A. Change plans only if it is possible to notify my parents.
	2B. Return home by curfew.
	2C. Ask permission, 2 hours before curfew, for any overnight visits.
	2D. Follow probation rules while socializing (no drinking or taking drugs).
3. Scheduling when my chores are done	3A. Bring dirty clothes to the basement if I want them washed.
	3B. Put my own clothes away if I don't want them stored in the basement.
	3C. Wash the family dishes twice a week by 10:00 p.m. if I want to use the family's dishes myself.
4. Budgeting my money	4A. Keep records of how much I earn and spend.
	4B. Balance my budget.

Teen Signature _____ Date _____

Parent(s) Signature(s)_____ Date _____

EXERCISE 13

Understanding Alternative Parenting Arrangements

GOALS

To discuss alternative parenting arrangements to the nuclear, biological family (e.g., step-families, foster families, formal or informal adoption, group homes, residential centers) and the reasons for living in them.

ACTIVITY

1. In the first part of the exercise, the story "Carol Is in Foster Care" (see p. 75) is read and used to initiate discussions of alternative living situations. Themes to cover about placements include the reasons for alternative parenting arrangements and the role of alternative parenting arrangements in protecting the safety of children. Themes to cover about children include the fact that children don't choose their parents but they can choose whether they become parents themselves and what kind of parents they become and that children are lovable; it is a parenting issue, not a child issue, whether a child is receiving good parenting.

2. Girls who are presently living or imminently going to live with alternative caregivers can proceed to the second phase of this exercise. In this phase, they have real or simulated conversations with their past and present caregivers to determine the reasons behind any changes in their living situations.

   a. If a girl's emotional or physical safety might be jeopardized by direct conversations with her parents, then simulated ones should be substituted. Simulated phone calls can be an effective substitution for real conversations with parents. During a phone call the girl can ask her parents questions such as: "Why did you leave me?" "Why didn't you believe me when I told you. . . ?" "Why did you hit me. . . ?" The therapist (as parent) responds as accurately as possible, reflecting what the parental dynamics might have been. If the girl is skilled enough, and understands enough of her mother and father's strengths and limitations as parents, it may be appropriate to follow up these simulated conversations with real ones.

INDIVIDUAL THERAPY INSTRUCTIONS

1. The girl reads the story aloud.
2. The therapist initiates a discussion of the story.
3. The therapist and girl discuss her present living situation.

FAMILY THERAPY INSTRUCTIONS

1. The therapist carefully assesses when and if it is appropriate to have sessions with the child and the biological parents to go through this exercise. In some circumstances, involving foster parents or other caregivers in addition to, or instead of, the biological parents may be valuable, especially if there have been adjustment problems within these alternate living situations.

2. Differences in parenting style between past and present caregivers can be discussed when appropriate.

GROUP THERAPY INSTRUCTIONS

1. The therapist can select a girl to read the story to the group.

2. The group can then create a drama involving Carol. The therapist insures that each character in the drama expresses a theme listed in the activity description as she carries out her role.

3. After acting out the drama, the girls can be encouraged to share their personal experiences in alternative parenting situations and the therapist can underscore the exercise themes.

EXERCISE 13 HANDOUT

Carol Is in Foster Care

Directions: Read and discuss this story.

Carol is 12 years old. She moved in with Mr. and Mrs. Langley, her foster parents, as a result of being abandoned by her family 2 months ago. Before this, she had been living with her mother, father, and four brothers. Two months ago, Carol looked very depressed in school; her counselor had taken her aside and asked her what was wrong. After repeated questioning, Carol had burst into tears and told her counselor about the problems within her family. Carol said that she had been her father's favorite. He had sex with her almost every night. He did not seem to like her brothers or her mother; he was always beating them. The school counselor notified Child Protective Services (CPS). A CPS worker went to interview Carol's mother and father. Her father, on hearing the abuse charges, pushed the protective services worker aside and ran off. Her mother told Carol that she (her mother) would need to move to another trailer because her father had not paid any bills before leaving. Carol was temporarily placed in a foster home. She has been waiting to hear from her mother. She wants to go back home. She feels that it is her fault that her mother has lost their home and that her family probably hates her.

UNIT FIVE

Sexuality

These exercises facilitate discussions of the physical changes that occur during puberty, constructive and destructive body images, and sexual feelings. These issues are vital to victimized and neglected girls because these girls may have received little if any guidance from their parents about the changes that will happen or are already happening to their bodies and the influences these changes have on their attitudes toward themselves and their relationships with peers. In addition, abused individuals may have lost a sense of control over their own bodies and have distorted body images.

There are six exercises within this unit. The exercises which are most appropriate for a particular client will depend on her stage of physical development and sexual history. The first two exercises educate girls about the physical changes of puberty and the meaning of terms that refer to the body and sexual activities. The next two exercises encourage the development of a healthy body image. The last two exercises draw distinctions between nurturance, love, and lust. During these exercises, issues of self-abuse are raised. Girls who engage in dangerous levels of self-abuse/self-mutilation may be doing so during dissociation states. Dissociative girls may need individual and/or inpatient treatment to bring these dangerous symptoms under control.

Other important issues that can be incorporated into this unit, but which are not directly covered in the exercises, include the difference between sexual orientation and gender identity, and the differences between engaging in certain types of sexual behaviors and having a certain sexual orientation. These are issues that may be particularly relevant to victims of sexual abuse. If these topics are relevant to a specific girl, therapists should consider addressing these issues in individual sessions. Homophobia among the girls has interfered with the author constructively discussing these topics in family or group sessions.

The major obstacle to implementation of these exercises is that parents, even if their child has been sexually active, may reject sex education. The topics most likely to be considered taboo by parents are masturbation, birth control/safe sex, and homosexuality. One potential solution to this problem is to discuss with parents, in advance, the issues that will be raised during the exercises. For example, they can be shown the book *What's Happening to Me?* (Mayle, 1975) which describes, in a humorous format, the physical changes that occur during puberty. Most parents, after reading through this book, will agree to allow their girl to read the book during therapy. More cautious parents have been willing to read the book with their girl over the course of a family session rather than in individual or group treatment. As a last resort, the therapist can remove the pages that are most offensive to the parents, thereby providing the girl with a more censored version of the issues.

A second approach is to empower parents to provide the sex education themselves. In adult-only sessions, the parents' attitudes and beliefs are explored. The therapist treats these attitudes and beliefs with respect while encouraging parents to take a different or more flexible approach to imparting this information to their children. For example, parents may express the attitudes that talking about sex leads to promiscuity, that sexual impulses should just be ignored, that masturbation is self-mutilation, and so on. The therapist can show respect for the parents' views by assuring them that treatment sessions will emphasize the value of celibacy before marriage. However, the therapist can matter-of-factly stress that sexual urges are strong and that teenagers have little experience coping with them. If the parents want their children to be celibate, then treatment sessions will need to provide teens with many strategies for maintaining self-control.

Parental support for sex education may ebb and flow, or one parent may be supportive while the other sabotages. If an exercise is not progressing therapeutically, go on to exercises in other units. After further rapport building with parents, it is often possible to return successfully to the sex education exercises.

EXERCISE 14

Understanding the Physical Changes of Puberty

GOALS

To discuss the physical changes that occur in puberty and how these may influence a person's sense of self.

ACTIVITY

1. The girls, if they are able to read, take turns reading pages out of the book *What's Happening to Me?* (Mayle, 1975). To order from the publisher, contact Carol Publishing Group, 102 Enterprise Avenue, Secaucus, NJ 07094 or call (201) 866-0490.

   a. As the pages are read, the therapist initiates a discussion about private and nonprivate parts of the body and how girls feel about their bodies as a result of any physical or sexual abuse they may have undergone. Issues to emphasize include the following: people own their own bodies; while everyone goes through the changes of puberty, these changes are very special and important; and these physical changes often provoke feelings of confusion.

INDIVIDUAL THERAPY INSTRUCTIONS

1. The therapist and girl take turns reading pages of the book.
2. The therapist may need to give examples of the problems that have been faced by other girls who have been victimized or neglected to underscore for the girl that she is not the only one experiencing feelings of confusion or discomfort as she goes through puberty.

FAMILY THERAPY INSTRUCTIONS

1. The therapist should discuss with the parents, in advance, what will be covered during the session to insure that the exercise can be constructive.
2. The entire family or subsystems (mother-daughter, father-son, older sister-younger sister) can read the story together depending on what has been determined to be most appropriate for a particular family. Same-gender adult role models, who will matter-of-factly respond to questions that are raised by the book, are important. If, for example, fathers are unable or unwilling to participate in sessions with their sons, and the therapist is a female, it may be optimal to have a familiar male role model help facilitate the discussion. These issues are more complex when the identified client is a sexual abuse

victim. For example, if a boy has been raped by a man, he may be more open during these discussions if the therapist is female.

GROUP THERAPY INSTRUCTIONS

1. The girls take turns reading pages out of the book.
2. The therapist underscores that not everyone begins or ends the physical changes of puberty at the same time.
3. The therapist encourages the girls to share their feelings about their bodies.

EXERCISE 15

Understanding Sexual Slang

GOAL

To help girls understand the meaning of sexual words.

ACTIVITY

1. Girls are encouraged to shout out all of the slang words they have ever heard dealing with sex.
2. The meaning of each word is then explained.
3. The therapist insures that many sexual realms are covered, including names for body parts, expressions referring to sexual activities, and expressions referring to pregnancy and birth control.
4. The therapist needs to model a nonjudgmental, matter-of-fact attitude toward these topics.
5. Girls may initially find this activity very embarrassing. Humor can be an effective mechanism in making this an engaging and informative rather than an embarrassing or boring activity.

INDIVIDUAL THERAPY INSTRUCTIONS

1. In some homes, use of sexual terms is considered inappropriate. Thus, it is important to clarify for the girl the intent of the session. The therapist should also be prepared to discuss the goals of the session with the girl's caretaker either before or after the session.
2. The therapist will need to take an active participant role in generating slang terms.
3. The slang words can be written down instead of shouted out if this facilitates the girl's participation.

FAMILY THERAPY INSTRUCTIONS

1. This activity may be most successful when the parents and therapist meet first and practice the activity before involving the children. This gives the therapist an opportunity to desensitize parents to the topics that will be covered and empower them to feel they have important information to impart to their children. In this way the therapist also insures that the parents "know a lot of answers" so that their children can see them as valuable resources.

2. Parents take charge of sessions involving their children. The therapist acts as a facilitator and a "trap" defuser as children may try to embarrass or humiliate their parents rather than seek information constructively.

GROUP THERAPY INSTRUCTIONS

1. The girls are encouraged to shout out slang words.
2. In discussing the meaning of terms, the therapist will need to correct any misinformation that the girls provide each other without allowing an atmosphere of humiliation to build up.
3. If girls in the group have been sexually abused, this exercise may lead to flashbacks or heightened emotional stress. The therapist needs to carefully monitor the girls to determine if anyone needs individual attention.

EXERCISE 16

Identifying Constructive and Destructive Body Images

GOALS

To encourage the development of a healthy body image through helping girls identify any attitudes or behaviors that are destructive to a healthy body image, and to encourage the development of constructive attitudes and behaviors.

ACTIVITY

1. The therapist engages the girls in a routine of stretching exercises using soft background music. This routine should involve only mild exertion so that girls can talk, think, and exercise at the same time.

2. As everyone exercises, each girl describes what she likes and does not like about her appearance.

3. The therapist encourages girls to counter each other's self-criticism, points out universalities (such as the fact that no one is satisfied with their appearance), and encourages alternative attitudes, for example, that no one looks exactly like anyone else, and uniqueness is exciting and special.

4. If it does not spontaneously come up, the therapist should raise the issue of self-abuse. Everyone, including the therapist, gives an example of personal self-abuse. Examples of self-abuse can include smoking, drinking alcohol, not washing, self-inflicted wounds (head banging, wrist slashing), not eating properly (anorexia, bulimia), not getting enough sleep, and so on. Although girls can usually identify incidence of self-abuse, they often are unaware of their reasons for doing it. The following possibilities can be discussed: Self-abuse may be self-infliction of injuries previously undergone at the hands of an abuser, or it may express self-hatred resulting from prior abuse and/or self-punishment for having undergone abuse.

INDIVIDUAL THERAPY INSTRUCTIONS

1. The therapist may need to broaden the discussion by having the girl critique not only her own appearance but that of her peers, her friends, movie stars, other members of the therapeutic staff, and so forth. An obstacle to this discussion is that it can easily become a lecture that the girl ignores.

2. In raising the issue of self-abuse, the therapist needs to be creative in thinking through and presenting realistic examples of personal self-abuse in order to facilitate accurate self-disclosure from the girl. With teenage girls, examples of famous

83

people who have self-abused may have more impact than examples of the therapist's own behavior.

FAMILY THERAPY INSTRUCTIONS

1. The therapist needs to consider whether it is more appropriate to discuss these issues with or without the exercising. The exercise format may be particularly valuable for families that need practice doing playful activities together.
2. Family members should try to help each other accurately assess their own body image and come up with examples of self-abuse. The therapist needs to assess, in advance, if it is appropriate for parents to discuss any ongoing self-abuse in front of their children. When this is not appropriate, examples from their teenage years may be effective substitutions.
3. It is important for the therapist to emphasize healthy parent-child boundaries.

   a. Parents should help their children stop self-abuse.
   b. Parents should get help from other adults to stop their own self-abuse.

GROUP THERAPY INSTRUCTIONS

1. The girls can exercise in a circle formation: Each girl, in order, can self-disclose.
2. A major obstacle to this activity is that teen girls may develop an alliance against the therapist in support of an anorexic body image and encourage each other in fad dieting. Autobiographical accounts of famous actresses or rock stars who have overcome bulimia or anorexia may be effective in countering these destructive teen norms.

EXERCISE 17

Building a Constructive Body Image

GOALS

To deepen the discussions begun in the earlier exercises with a greater emphasis on the substitution of constructive for destructive behaviors.

ACTIVITY

1. The girls demonstrate stretching exercises that are then put together into a new routine.
2. During this routine, the therapist initiates a review of the issues raised in the earlier exercise. Girls are encouraged to talk about any abuse or neglect of their bodies, specifically about how it affected their comfort with and attitudes toward their bodies. Abuse victims often feel their bodies are dirty or bad, or do not belong to themselves. These feelings should be validated; however, they are misperceptions that need to be countered strongly by the therapist. Everyone's body has "a right" to be cared for and respected.
3. This exercise should end with each girl making a commitment to being good to her body by engaging in good grooming, seeking appropriate medical and dental care, eating healthy foods, and getting proper exercise. Enhanced personal care when one is feeling bad, such as taking a warm bath or putting on favorite clothing, can be encouraged as substitutions for self-abuse or neglect.

INDIVIDUAL THERAPY INSTRUCTIONS

1. While progressing through the activity, the therapist needs to bring up examples of how abuse has affected the body image of other girls to aid the client in understanding her own dynamics.
2. The girl should leave the session with her own list of strategies for avoiding destructive behaviors and substituting constructive ones.

FAMILY THERAPY INSTRUCTIONS

1. The therapist needs to carefully evaluate which family members to include in this activity.
2. Direct family discussions may be more appropriate than an exercise format.
3. Family members can be encouraged to come up with both individual and family plans for improving their body images. Therapists need to insure that family plans respect

appropriate parent-child boundaries. For example, it would be appropriate for a girl to ask her mother for help blow-drying her hair when she is feeling self-abusive. However, a mother who feels self-abusive should turn to other adults, not to her children, for help.

GROUP THERAPY INSTRUCTIONS

1. The girls exercise in a circle formation to facilitate peer interactions.
2. The therapist should encourage the development of positive peer pressure to help members overcome self-abusive behavior.
3. The girls can help each other brainstorm constructive replacements for self-abusive behavior.

EXERCISE 18

Comparing Nurturance, Love, and Lust

GOALS

To discuss the relationships between nurturance, love, and lust.

ACTIVITY

1. The therapist hands out poems, cartoons, wise sayings, and so on, from Sol Gordon's *The Teenage Survival Book* that pertain to "How to tell if you're really in love" (1981) for girls to use in comparing and contrasting nurturance, love, and lust. To order from the publisher, contact Random House, Westminster Distribution Center, 400 Hahn Road, Westminster, MD 21157 or call (800) 733-3000. The therapist stresses the following points:

   a. You can experience strong sexual feelings for people with whom you have nothing in common.
   b. Strong sexual feelings can come on suddenly and be very transitory.
   c. Experiencing mutual lust with someone does not imply that the relationship will last or be healthy for you.
   d. "Real" romantic love includes a combination of nurturance, understanding, and lust.

INDIVIDUAL THERAPY INSTRUCTIONS

1. The therapist should be aware that the girl may ask personal questions about the therapist's own sexual experiences and should consider in advance how to respond to these questions. The therapist does not want to fall into the trap of saying sexual experiences are too personal to share; this gives the girl a reason not to share either.
2. The therapist should plan in advance how to handle a revelation by the girl that she is sexually active.

FAMILY THERAPY INSTRUCTIONS

1. The therapist may need to rehearse this exercise in an adults-only session prior to having family sessions to insure that the parents have thought about the difference between lust and love.

   a. People may marry because of unanticipated pregnancies and justify this course of events to themselves on the basis of "true love." When teens ask these parents how to know if it is the right time for sex and other intimacies, these parents may say, "It will feel right"; "You will know"; and so forth. Going through the exercise in parental sessions first, and working sensitively through these issues, will be an important step before putting the parents in charge of the exercise in a family session.

2. Once the parents are ready, have them hand out the materials and facilitate the discussion. The therapist needs to insure that the sessions proceed constructively, because children may ask some questions just to embarrass their parents.
3. Appropriate adult-child boundaries need to be stressed, especially in families where there has been sexual abuse.

GROUP THERAPY INSTRUCTIONS

1. Hand out a different cartoon, wise saying, or poem to each girl and then have each one in turn lead a discussion of what they have been given.
2. The girls may seek to embarrass each other or the therapist and/or provide destructive advice to each other. The therapist needs to help the girls consider the pros and cons of different sexual choices without directly condemning a girl's suggestions (unless it involves abusive behavior).

EXERCISE 19

Understanding the Consequences of Sexual Behavior

GOALS

To discuss the responsibilities and dangers involved in engaging in sexual behaviors.

ACTIVITY

1. The therapist hands out poems, wise sayings, cartoons, and so on, from Gordon (1981) dealing with pregnancy, sexually transmitted diseases, and acquired immunodeficiency syndrome (AIDS) to facilitate a discussion of the consequences of sexual behavior. To order from the publisher, contact Random House, Westminster Distribution Center, 400 Hahn Road, Westminster, MD 21157 or call (800) 733-3000.

2. The therapist should underscore that one can enjoy sexual feelings without engaging in sexual behaviors, and that comfort with one's sexuality is something that builds up over time.

INDIVIDUAL THERAPY INSTRUCTIONS

1. The therapist should carefully adjust this activity to fit the needs of the girl. Depending on prior experience (consensual or nonconsensual sex, etc.) and the timing of puberty, different girls will be ready to process varying amounts of information on these topics at different times.

2. The girl and therapist can create some of their own cartoons and wise sayings to reflect the girl's current level of sexual interest. The therapist can foreshadow, for the girl, issues that may soon become important to her.

FAMILY THERAPY INSTRUCTIONS

1. The therapist needs to carefully consider whether parental practice sessions are needed prior to family sessions. The most effective family sessions will occur if the parents can be empowered to use their own personal experience to help their children make careful, well-thought-out choices. Parents need to understand that showing acceptance of a child's sexual feelings is not incompatible with encouraging a child to be celibate.

2. Appropriate adult-child boundaries need to be stressed, especially in families where there has been sexual abuse.

GROUP THERAPY INSTRUCTIONS

1. Hand out a different cartoon, wise saying, or poem to each girl and have them take turns leading a discussion of what they have been given. The therapist should be aware that teens, due to egocentric thought and myths of invulnerability, frequently discount dangers to themselves. Important messages, such as about AIDS, may be most effectively addressed through peers and concern for peers. Providing examples of teens and teen role models the girls have heard of who have contracted AIDS before discussing issues such as "safe sex" may engender greater motivation to absorb the messages.

Physical Victimization

These exercises provide basic information about the dynamics of spousal violence and child physical abuse. Exercises focused on these issues are important because witnesses and/or participants in family violence are at high risk for the development of both internalizing (passive) and externalizing (aggressive) behaviors (Jaffe, Wolfe, & Wilson, 1990). Through educating girls about the negative impact of family violence and encouraging them to substitute nurturance for aggression in family interactions, the development of prosocial competencies within family members becomes more likely (Berman, 1993).

The four exercises in this unit stress the negative impact of family violence and detail the response styles of abusers and victims. Exercises 20 and 21 are specific to spousal violence, and exercises 22 and 23 are specific to child abuse.

The responsibility of parents for protecting and caring for their children should be highlighted throughout the exercises. Even when teaching escape strategies, children should never be given the impression that they are responsible for ending family violence or protecting themselves; ending violence is an adult responsibility. Information about the patterns of violence and how they change over time can be included in the exercises when appropriate. For example, spousal violence may progress from mild to life-endangering incidents. The pattern of child abuse is not the same for all families, and the pattern within a particular family may change over time. Abuse patterns can include abuse that begins in early childhood (or even infancy) and continues throughout adolescence, physical punishment in early years that escalates to physical abuse in adolescence, physical abuse that occurs only at ages when children are most prone to contrariness (toddlers, teens), and abuse that erupts for the first time in the teen years (U.S. Department of Health and Human Services, 1980).

A major concern regarding the safe implementation of these exercises is the differential power that frequently exists within families. Nonabusive parents may be in personal danger if they attempt to intervene between the abusive parent and the child victim. Likewise, nonviolent spouses may be in danger when they attempt to mediate the behavior of the violent spouse. Therapists need to carefully assess the level of dangerousness in the home to determine when and to whom these exercises should be introduced. Issues of safety must be successfully addressed in treatment before interpersonal growth can become an appropriate goal. Potential solutions to this problem of differential power involve either permanent or temporary separation of the family from the violent individual to insure the safety of other family members. The victimization exercises can be implemented separately with the nonviolent and violent family members, or they can be worked through with the family as a whole, provided the violence is under control and the therapist carefully monitors individuals for stress reactions. Family members may have confused feelings about each other and the violent episodes. For example, children often engage in either/or thinking (if they love their abusive parent, then they must tolerate that parent's abusive behavior; likewise, if they report the abuse, then they can't love their parent). The therapist needs to engender comfort with an attitude that separates the person from the behavior (e.g., it's okay to love the abusive parent but consider the violent behavior unacceptable).

EXERCISE 20

Recognizing Spouse Abuse Dynamics

GOALS

To stimulate an awareness of the inappropriateness of spousal violence and indicate its negative impact on children.

ACTIVITY

1. Girls read and respond to the content of the story "Cathy Was Scared" (see p. 95).
2. The therapist can facilitate the discussion by asking questions such as what happened, who started it, who ended it, and how it affected the family members. Important information to weave into the discussion includes the prevalence of violence within families and the typical escalation of violence from mild to severe (e.g., from threatening, to hitting, to using a dangerous weapon). The therapist should stress that violence is never an acceptable way to deal with family conflict, and that adults are responsible for ending violence within the family.
3. When appropriate, this discussion can be followed up with information about assessing dangerousness, developing escape strategies, and petitioning for a protection order. The booklet by the Channing L. Bete Co. (1979) can be handed out to girls or used by the therapist as a source of ideas for stimulating further discussions. To order this booklet, contact Channing L. Bete Co., Inc., 200 State Road, South Deerfield, MA 01373 or call (800) 628-7733.

INDIVIDUAL THERAPY INSTRUCTIONS

1. The therapist should modify the story in advance to parallel, but not be equivalent to, the dynamics within the girl's family.
2. The girl reads the story aloud and then discusses it with the therapist.
3. After the story, if the girl is ready, the discussion can begin to focus on the girl's own situation.

FAMILY THERAPY INSTRUCTIONS

1. The therapist must exercise caution in determining if and when to include an abusive parent within this activity.
2. A family member, preferably a supportive adult, reads the story aloud.
3. The therapist and supportive adult act as cofacilitators when the story is discussed. They take turns asking questions about the story and try to develop a consensus

within the family about the negative impact of violence on family members. Safety themes and adult-child boundaries need to be stressed.

4. After discussing the story, a direct discussion of the family's current situation may be possible. The therapist must assess the appropriateness and readiness of each family for such discussions; the physical safety of family members must be a primary consideration. The development of appropriate parent-child boundaries should be emphasized when applicable.

5. If a violent family member is maintaining contact with the family, a nitty-gritty family assessment of the relative dangerousness of this individual is necessary, and a family protection plan needs to be developed.

GROUP THERAPY INSTRUCTIONS

1. The therapist selects a group member to read the story.
2. During the discussion, different opinions about why the violence is happening in Cathy's family and how different family members may be feeling should be highlighted and validated. To encourage disclosures, the therapist should indicate, in a neutral voice, the commonness of violence within families. However, the therapist also needs to take an unequivocal stance against the use of violence within families.

EXERCISE 20 HANDOUT

Cathy Was Scared

Directions: _Read and discuss this story._

Cathy was sleeping one night when all of a sudden she woke up with a start. The house seemed full of thumping and shouting. She sat up in bed and listened. Mom and Dad were having another fight. Cathy's door was shut so she couldn't hear everything that was being said. She could hear her dad calling her mother names, but she couldn't hear what her mother was saying. Then she began to hear even scarier sounds. Cathy was scared. She was thinking that her mother might get hurt or killed and that she wanted to help but was too afraid to move. She hid under her blanket, but she was still scared and she could still hear the noises. So she got out of bed and went to the door. She opened it and called out, "Mom, Dad, I'm having nightmares, I'm so scared." The noises stopped. Cathy called out again "Mom, Dad, please come quick." Cathy heard the front door slam and then the steps of someone coming up the stairs. Cathy ran back to bed and pulled the covers around her. Cathy's mom came into the room. Her mom looked terrible. She came over to Cathy and gave her a big hug. Cathy and her mom hugged each other for a long time. Then Cathy's mom turned off the light and left the room.

EXERCISE 21

Recognizing Children's Reactions to Spouse Abuse

GOALS

To help girls recognize and gain insight into children's reactions to family violence.

ACTIVITY

1. In Step 1, the girls are told that children may have many different types of thoughts and behave in many different ways after witnessing parental violence, and that some of these thoughts and ways of behaving are listed in a handout. The therapist gives each girl a copy of the handout, "After Seeing a Fight Between My Parents I . . ."(p. 99; adapted from Beckford & Berman, 1992). The girls then read through the list and discuss each of these reactions to family violence in terms of the benefits and/or disadvantages it brings to the child, including how the reaction may be viewed by significant others (teachers, friends, police, etc.). For example, the therapist could ask how likely it is that a specific reaction will lead someone to help the child, result in the child being punished, result in the child being physically hurt, result in the child being ignored, prevent the child from achieving in school, or prevent the child from making friends.

2. In Step 2, girls look through the response list again, this time for examples of passive, aggressive, and active behavior.

   a. The therapist may need to give concrete definitions of passive, aggressive, and active behavior.
   b. The therapist helps the girls think through which general response style brings the most advantages (e.g., personal safety, personal growth) to the girl.

3. In Step 3, the girls identify the type of behavior the children in their family are most likely to exhibit after a violent episode. Girls identify what response style (passive, aggressive, active) their behavior represents. Alternative responses to these episodes, that might result in greater benefits to the children, can then be explored, underscoring that it is the responsibility of adults to stop family violence.

INDIVIDUAL THERAPY INSTRUCTIONS

1. The therapist and girl go through the list together.

2. The specific dynamics of the girl's family and her reaction to these dynamics should be highlighted. The therapist needs to interject comments about how the girl's specific responses to violence are helping or interfering with her personal development.

FAMILY THERAPY INSTRUCTIONS

1. The therapist needs to carefully assess if a family is ready for this activity.
2. After discussing each reaction in the list, the family members should consider which type of reaction (passive, aggressive, active) most closely mimics their own style. Family members can be expected to have developed differential responses to violence. The reasons behind their differing styles can be discussed as well as the advantages and disadvantages of these styles.

GROUP THERAPY INSTRUCTIONS

1. The group can be divided into teams of three or four people.
2. Each team goes through Steps 1 and 2 separately. Within a team, it is not necessary for the girls to reach a consensus about the benefits or advantages of every individual reaction discussed in Step 1. However, in Step 2, the therapist should attempt to help the girls reach a consensus as to whether passive, aggressive, or active response styles *in general* bring the most advantages to the girl.
3. If the girls have not already begun discussing their personal reactions to parental violence, initiate Step 3.
4. After Step 3 is completed, the therapist should draw attention to similarities and differences in response styles across group members. Peer support should be generated for helping individuals move toward active behavior.

EXERCISE 21 HANDOUT

After Seeing a Fight Between My Parents I . . .

1. did mean things to people.

2. talked to my teacher or counselor about it.

3. had headaches.

4. called the police.

5. left the house because I didn't want to hear it.

6. tried to hurt myself.

7. took it out on my dog (pet).

8. called an adult family member to help stop the fight.

9. hid because I was so scared.

10. broke something to distract them.

11. talked to my friends about it.

12. jumped into the fight.

13. didn't pay attention in school.

14. had trouble sleeping.

15. felt like there was nothing I could do about it.

16. felt shaky and nervous all over.

17. screamed and yelled at them.

18. ignored them because they fight all the time.

19. felt sick.

EXERCISE 22

Understanding Child Abuser Dynamics

GOALS

To discuss the dynamics behind abuser and victim behavior.

ACTIVITY

Part 1

1. In Part 1, the girls read the story "Parenting a Young Child" (see p. 103).
2. The therapist elicits responses to the following questions:

   a. Why did the parent do what she did?
   b. Why did the child do what she did?
   c. What should be done about the situation?

3. Important themes to highlight during these discussions include:

   a. Most parents who abuse their children want to be good parents and want their children to be happy and successful.
   b. Some physical abusers are not interested in being good parents and derive satisfaction from the pain they inflict on children.
   c. Child abuse is never acceptable behavior.

Part 2

1. In Part 2, the therapist begins a discussion of how abuse may start within a family, stressing that, over time, the dynamics of abuse within a family may change. For example, abuse that began due to ignorance of normal child development (as in the story "Parenting a Young Child") may become abuse due to an atmosphere of mutual parent-child hostility.
2. The girls then try to think through how the abuse started within their own family. If girls develop an understanding of the dynamics that first initiated the abuse, they may develop more flexibility in responding to their present family situation.
3. The therapist can use information from the booklet by the Channing L. Bete Co. (1989) for further ideas to incorporate into discussions of child abuse. To order this booklet,

contact Channing L. Bete Co., Inc., 200 State Road, South Deerfield, MA 01373 or call (800) 628-7733.

INDIVIDUAL THERAPY INSTRUCTIONS

1. The therapist can modify the story to parallel features of the girl's family life if the family dynamics when the abuse first began are known.
2. Proceed with Parts 1 and 2 of the activity using the modified or unmodified story.

FAMILY THERAPY INSTRUCTIONS

1. Have a family member read the story aloud, then proceed with Part 1 of the activity.
2. Attempts should be made to engender empathy among family members for both the mother and the child.
3. The therapist should insure that by the end of Part 1, family members realize that the parent-child conflict was a result of the mother's lack of understanding of normal child development. The therapist should underscore that this is a common dynamic in incidents of child abuse.
4. The therapist may want to proceed with Part 2 of the activity with only the parents present; this may be advisable to insure that this step is not an emotionally abusive experience for either the parents or the children. The therapist can help the parents recall the earliest incidents of abuse within their home and try to reconstruct the dynamics underlying it. The therapist should help each spouse empathize with the difficulties that the other faced in parenting. The need for alternatives to violent parenting strategies should be stressed.
5. Once Part 2 has been successful with the parents alone, the children can be brought in and this part repeated. If discussions of early abuse episodes are constructive, the family can begin to trace the pattern of abuse over time until the present and try to understand the reasons behind the changes in family behavior.

GROUP THERAPY INSTRUCTIONS

1. One girl should read the story aloud to the group, and then the group can proceed through Parts 1 and 2 of the activity.
2. In discussing the parent's behavior in Part 1, the therapist should underscore that not all family violence occurs for the same reasons.
3. In carrying through Part 2, the therapist should stress that it is not safe for all children to continue living at home while their families learn to live a nonviolent lifestyle.
4. The therapist should carefully monitor the girls for stress reactions. Peer support should be encouraged to help girls recognize they are not alone and they are not "bad" because they come from violent homes.

EXERCISE 22 HANDOUT

Parenting a Young Child

__Directions:__ Read and discuss the story.

Judy is 17 years old. Her daughter Michelle is 1½. Judy is at the emergency room of the hospital with Michelle; this is the fourth time this year. This time, Michelle has a large bruise on her face. Judy is very frustrated with, and worried about, Michelle. The nurse asks Judy what happened. After some initial denial, Judy says that she hit Michelle because Michelle had been so stubborn and disobedient. Judy had been working with Michelle every day for the last week to teach her the names of colors. She would hold up two crayons and say, "This is blue; this is green." Then, after a few repetitions, she would tell her to "Reach for the blue crayon," and so on. She said that teaching Michelle had been very slow and frustrating, but that she had not given up because she wanted Michelle to do well in school. Yesterday, she had been very excited because Michelle had, finally, learned the names for blue and green. Judy knew that Michelle understood these words because twice in a row when she had asked her to reach for the blue crayon, Michelle had done it correctly. Today, she had been planning to begin working on red and orange but had started with blue and green again just to remind Michelle how to do the activity correctly. When Judy had asked her to reach for the blue crayon, Michelle had reached for the green one. This happened several times even though she told Michelle to stop fooling around. In retelling this story, Judy became angry. She was tired of working so hard to help Michelle; her daughter was ungrateful and lazy!

EXERCISE 23

Developing Constructive
Parent-Child Relationships

GOALS

To help clients identify the different ways children may respond to parental authority and to encourage the development of constructive strategies.

ACTIVITY

Part 1

1. In Part 1, the girls read and discuss the "Responding to Parental Authority Scenarios" (see p. 107). For each scenario, they discuss what the problem was, how the parent tried to solve the problem, and how the child tried to solve the problem.
2. Important issues to stress, after all of the scenarios have been discussed, are that children may be abused for reasons that have nothing to do with their own behavior and that, even if a child intentionally aggravates a parent, it is never acceptable for a parent to respond with violence.

Part 2

1. In Part 2, girls generate alternative strategies for resolving the conflict reflected in the scenarios that involve assertive communication and maintain appropriate parent-child boundaries.

INDIVIDUAL THERAPY INSTRUCTIONS

1. The therapist and girl take turns reading the scenarios as they go through the first part of the activity.
2. In generating alternatives in the second part of the activity, the therapist should stress that it may not be safe to use assertive skills with some people. The child should be encouraged to engage in realistic self-protective strategies in dangerous situations.

FAMILY THERAPY INSTRUCTIONS

1. In Part 1, family members take turns reading the scenarios. The therapist helps the parent take charge of the discussions of each scenario. The therapist should help engender empathy for both the parental and child positions without condoning the use of violence by anyone for solving problems.

2. The therapist helps the parent lead Part 2 of the activity.

GROUP THERAPY INSTRUCTIONS

1. The girls can take turns reading the scenarios in Part 1 of the activity. Different girls may identify with varying response styles; it is important that an atmosphere of constructive analysis, rather than ridicule, be maintained.

2. For Part 2, it may be helpful to break down into teams, assigning a few scenarios to each team. Each team develops a constructive strategy for resolving the conflict in each of their scenarios. The teams can take turns either reading or acting out their new strategies for the group as a whole.

EXERCISE 23 HANDOUT

Responding to
Parental Authority Scenarios

Directions: Read and discuss the scenarios.

1. Nancy was lying on the couch watching MTV. Her mother stood in the doorway and watched her for a minute. Nancy did not look up. Her mother then told her to get up and clean her room. Nancy ignored her. Her mother switched off the TV. Nancy used the remote control to turn it back on. Mom pulled Nancy off the couch and dragged her out of the room.

2. Judy was washing dishes. Her father came in and asked her where her brother was. Judy looked up and said that he had left the house a few minutes ago. Her father called her a stupid fool for letting him leave and grabbed her by the arm. She apologized. He flung her on the floor and kicked her before leaving the house.

3. Becky came home from the mall with a bag full of new clothes. Her father asked her to show him the sales receipt. She hugged the bag to her stomach and told him to mind his own business. He demanded that she tell him where she had gotten the money to buy the clothes. She swore at him and tried to run past him to her room. He grabbed her by the arm and asked her if she had been stealing again. She slapped him. He slammed her against the wall.

4. Patty was doing her homework when she heard her mother come in the house. As she heard the door slam, she quickly turned down the music in her room. Her mother burst in. Patty told her mom that she had put the other kids to bed and had dinner waiting. While serving dinner to her mom, Patty asked what had happened to make her mom so mad. Patty's mom began to tell her about her day at work.

UNIT SEVEN

Sexual Victimization

The goal of these activities is to help girls take control over their past experiences of sexual abuse through understanding the differential power between the adult abuser and the child victim in terms of position of authority in the family, larger physical size, and greater knowledge of the world. These exercises are important because victims typically do not fully understand what has happened to them. They blame themselves for the abuse and are intimidated, sometimes even into adulthood, by their abusers. The long-term impact on victims of untreated sexual abuse has included alcohol and/or drug abuse, suicidal behavior, participation in abusive relationships, eating disorders, flashbacks, and so on (Swink & Leveille, 1986).

Four exercises are provided. The first two focus on the dynamics of the abuser, and the second two focus on the dynamics of the victim. The intent of these exercises is to lead girls, at a pace they can tolerate, into personal disclosures and processing of their own victimization. Initial disclosures should be kept to a minimum. Over time, larger amounts of disclosure can be tolerated by the girls without stress levels becoming too high for a therapeutic experience. After completing these four exercises, most girls will be ready to continue processing their own experiences.

Over time, important auxiliary issues to discuss include reactions of siblings, grandparents, and nonabusive parental figures to the child's victimization; the reasons that family members may or may not be supporting the victim's allegations; reactions of school teachers and peers if the abusive events have been publicized; and how to decide when and if to tell more people (adults, friends) about the victimization. The chapter "Family Secrets" (Karpel & Strauss, 1983) can be an important source of ideas for the therapist during these discussions.

The major obstacle to successful completion of these exercises is the high stress level they generate. A potential solution is to break these exercises into 15-minute segments of discussion followed by 15 minutes of relaxation. Controlled breathing is an easy relaxation technique to use. The girls are told to inhale and exhale to the count of four which is repeated slowly by the therapist. The girls raise a hand when they can hear their heartbeat. When all the girls are hearing their hearts, they will be relatively relaxed. After a few minutes of experiencing this relaxed feeling, the girls can go back to the exercises.

More sophisticated forms of relaxation exercises can be used if controlled breathing does not provide enough relief from anxiety.

In family treatment, children younger than 9 may have difficulty concentrating during relaxation exercises and, thus, may not benefit from them. For these children, a breathing contest may be more effective in reducing anxiety levels. Children are told to hold their breath as long as possible. When they must breathe, they are told to expel the air making the funniest noise they can. While this exercise doesn't promote physical relaxation *per se*, it usually promotes psychological relaxation, because children make such crazy noises that family members usually start laughing. If stress levels are still too high for constructive discussions, the family can engage in silly games (Berman, 1992).

Another obstacle to these exercises is that reading is required; some of the family members may have limited reading skills due to young age, poor school attendance, or learning disabilities. A potential solution is to have the therapist, another family member, or another girl help when reading difficulties arise, or give the person with reading difficulties another role in the activity.

EXERCISE 24

Recognizing Abuser Strategies

GOAL

To discuss some common ways sexual abusers manipulate children.

ACTIVITY

1. A discussion about how to "know your abuser" is initiated through using the handout, "Recognizing Abuser Strategies" (p. 113). The issues detailed in this handout are covered more thoroughly in Sgroi (1985).
2. Each girl receives a copy of the handout, and the therapist starts a discussion about each line, asking the girls to come up with further examples of each strategy and encouraging the girls to discuss which of the strategies have relevance for them.
3. Some important messages to get across about abusers are that (a) whatever their strategy, they cared only for themselves and not about the welfare of their child victims; (b) the abusers took advantage of the children and used the strategy they thought would work; (c) if one strategy did not work, the abusers would have tried another until a strategy was found that did work; and (d) abusers may be family members, familiar adults (older children, teens), or strangers.
4. Some important messages to get across about victims are that (a) children need to protect themselves - not their abusers; (b) child victims had no choice, only, perhaps, the illusion of choice; and (c) standing up for themselves would have terminated their abuse only if the abusers had found an easier victim or if the abusers had found themselves in danger of being caught.
5. If the discussion generated by this activity is superficial, or the girls request more information on why people become sexual abusers, go on to Exercise 25.

INDIVIDUAL THERAPY INSTRUCTIONS

1. The therapist and the girl take turns reading a line of the handout and bringing up further examples of each strategy.
2. The girl should be helped to identify the strategies that had been used on her. The therapist should confirm for the girl that these strategies were manipulative and that many other girls have been manipulated by them in the past.
3. The therapist can provide concrete examples of strategies that had been used on other children that were both more and less damaging than those used on the girl.

This can help give the girl a sense of hope in fighting the "damaged goods syndrome" (e.g., others have been hurt even worse and have survived).

FAMILY THERAPY INSTRUCTIONS

1. The therapist should conduct family sessions only if the nonabusive parent is showing signs of being supportive of the child victim. It will be a rare family that can include the sexual abuser in the session and proceed constructively.

2. The therapist and family members take turns reading a line of the handout and try to identify the strategies that were used in their family. Some siblings, for example, will have resented the abused sibling because they only perceived the enticements/bribes the abuser offered the child and were not aware of the price the abuser extracted for these enticements. The nonabusive parent may have misinterpreted enticements as incidences of positive parenting. It may be revealed that more than one child within the family was abused, but that each, due to the conspiracy of silence imposed by the abuser, thought that they were alone and isolated.

3. The therapist will need to clearly tie together cause and effect for the family members. For example, the abuser did not take the child to the park to be a good nuturer, but rather, to place the child under a sense of obligation so that sexual activity could be demanded of them later as a payback.

GROUP THERAPY INSTRUCTIONS

1. Sitting in a circle, each girl takes a turn reading a line of the handout; members of the group are encouraged to come up with further examples of each strategy.

2. Girls are encouraged to share with the group examples that are relevant to their own victimization.

3. The therapist must carefully monitor each girl's reaction to the exercise. Girls who have been sexually abused may show stress reactions. Girls who have not been sexually abused may make insensitive, pejorative comments.

EXERCISE 24 HANDOUT

Recognizing Abuser Strategies

Directions: ***Read and discuss.***

**WAYS THE ABUSER GETS YOU INVOLVED IN SEX;
THEY ALL INVOLVE FORCING YOU**

1. Enticement Strategies

    a. Bribery: "If you do this for me, I'll give you a reward."
    b. Game: "Let me teach you this fun game."

2. Entrapment Strategies

    a. Making you feel obligated using guilt: "You have to do this for me because you owe me."
    b. Making you feel obligated using fear: "If you do not do this for me, I will have to tell that you are smoking."

3. Verbal Threats

    a. Threat of harm to the child: "You're really going to get it."
    b. Threat of harm to the abuser: "If you tell, I'll go to jail."
    c. Threat of withdrawal of affection: "If you don't, I won't love you anymore."
    d. Threat of family breaking up: "This would really hurt your mom."
    e. Threat to loved ones: "I'll hurt your mother if you don't do it."

4. Use of Physical Force

**THINGS ABUSERS OFTEN SAY WHICH TAKE ADVANTAGE OF CHILDREN'S
LACK OF KNOWLEDGE AND THEIR DEPENDENCY ON ADULTS**

1. "It's okay - everybody does it."
2. "I'm just checking you out, now that you're getting older."
3. "What's the matter? Don't you like me?"

EXERCISE 25

Understanding Sexual Abuser Dynamics

GOAL

To deepen the discussion of sexual abuser dynamics begun in Exercise 24.

ACTIVITY

1. The girls take turns reading from the chapter "Understanding People Who Sexually Abuse Children" (Daugherty, 1984). You can order this book from your local bookstore or directly from the publisher. To order from the publisher, contact Mother Courage Press, 1667 Douglas Avenue, Racine, WI 53404-2721 or call 414-637-2227. The strength of this chapter is that it describes in detail different patterns of perpetrator behavior and abuse. The weakness is that it is extremely explicit and highly stressful. Therefore, it might be most appropriate to edit this chapter, providing only the information that is specifically relevant to each girl.

2. Girls are encouraged to identify which dynamics most closely represent the behavior of their abuser.

3. Stress reactions from the girls need to be expected, monitored, and adequately responded to by the therapist.

INDIVIDUAL THERAPY INSTRUCTIONS

1. The therapist and girl take turns reading from the chapter.

2. As they discuss the girl's abuser, the therapist should help the girl understand what factors may have led the person to become an abuser.

   a. It is important not to engender pity for the abuser but, rather, to clarify for the girl that it was the dynamics of the abuser that lead to the girl's victimization, not her dynamics.

FAMILY THERAPY INSTRUCTIONS

1. The therapist should conduct family sessions only if the nonabusive parent is showing signs of being supportive of the child victim. It will be a rare family that can include the sexual abuser in the session and proceed constructively.

2. The therapist, and those members of the family with good reading skills, can take turns reading the chapter.

3. Younger family members may have trouble understanding the material. The therapist should empower the nonabusive parent to help the younger children understand the material. The therapist can use these events as opportunities to underscore the naïveté of children in comparison to adults and the relative ease with which adults can teach children either adaptive or maladaptive skills. Any member of the family may undergo a stress reaction in response to this material. For example, nonabusive parents may suddenly realize how they inadvertently supported the abuse.

GROUP THERAPY INSTRUCTIONS

1. It is recommended that there be at least two therapists present before initiating this activity in a group because more than one girl may experience a crisis reaction during this exercise.
2. The girls sit in a circle and take turns reading from the chapter and discussing the information it provides.
3. The therapists carefully monitor the group for stress reactions. The stress reaction of a girl who is quietly compliant may be overlooked if there is another girl overtly weeping. If necessary, one therapist can temporarily leave group with a girl to give her individual attention. If a girl has a significant stress reaction, in addition to providing therapist and peer support within a session, follow-up contacts should be made later in the day and/or week to monitor her welfare. These checkup phone calls can be discussed in group so that the girls know when they can expect further support.

EXERCISE 26

Understanding Sexual Abuse Victim Dynamics

GOAL

To discuss the dynamics of sexual abuse victims.

ACTIVITY

1. Girls take turns reading from the book *No More Secrets for Me* (Wachter, 1983). This book contains four short stories about sexual abuse. Each one involves a different situation, and they become progressively more stressful. You can order this book from your local bookstore or directly from the publisher. To order from the publisher, contact Little, Brown and Company, Inc., 200 West Street, Waltham, MA 02154 or call (800) 343-9204.

2. As each story is read, the therapist facilitates a discussion of the feelings and experiences of the characters in the story. Any self-disclosures of abuse from girls can be integrated into the discussion, but there should be no pressure to disclose. As the stories are being read, the therapist can initiate discussions of what the stories have in common, such as how the victim felt or actions the victim realistically could have taken.

3. It is recommended that only one story be read per session. The following themes should be stressed in summarizing information across stories:

   a. Sexually abused children often feel guilty and sad because they think the abuse was their fault.
   b. Adults trick children and make them believe they cooperated.
   c. When an adult touches a child sexually, it sometimes feels good to the child. This is not unusual and does not make the abuse the child's fault.
   e. Adults should never involve a child in sexual activities.

4. If the discussion generated by these stories is superficial, or the girls do not seem ready to go on to direct discussions of their own victimization, go on to Exercise 27.

INDIVIDUAL THERAPY INSTRUCTIONS

1. The therapist and girl can take turns reading pages from each story. The therapist needs to help the girl see that she is not alone or unique in having been victimized by pointing out to her commonalities between her own experiences, those illustrated in the stories, and those of other girls seen by the therapist.

117

FAMILY THERAPY INSTRUCTIONS

1. The therapist needs to exercise caution in deciding which family members to include in this exercise. Family sessions can be helpful or destructive depending on whether they can engender emotional support for the victim. The therapist may need to have sessions alone with the nonabusive parent or parents to insure that later family sessions will be constructive. It will be a rare family that can include a sexually abusive parent and proceed through this exercise constructively.

GROUP THERAPY INSTRUCTIONS

1. The girls sit in a circle and take turns reading pages out of the book.
2. Group members will not necessarily know the details of each other's victimization prior to this exercise beginning, and they may unintentionally, or intentionally, make judgmental or insensitive remarks. The therapist needs to insure that each girl's feelings and experiences are validated and that no one feels scapegoated by the group.

EXERCISE 27

Answering Questions About Sexual Abuse

GOALS

To discuss common questions children pose about sexual abuse and help children think through their own abuse dynamics.

ACTIVITY

1. The girls read the chapter "Questions and Answers About Child Sexual Abuse" (Daugherty, 1984). Among the questions answered in the chapter are the following: What is abuse? What happens during abusive episodes? Who abuses children? What are the patterns of sexual abuse? As each of these questions is posed and answered, the girls can be encouraged to discuss how the information fits with their personal experiences. Individual differences should be validated. You can order this book from your local bookstore or directly from the publisher. To order from the publisher, contact Mother Courage Press, 1667 Douglas Avenue, Racine, WI 53404-2721 or call 414-637-2227.

INDIVIDUAL THERAPY INSTRUCTIONS

1. The therapist and girl read through the chapter together.
2. The therapist continues to raise the themes begun in earlier exercises that are most relevant to the girl.

FAMILY THERAPY INSTRUCTIONS

1. The therapist should continue working with whichever family members were deemed appropriate in earlier sexual abuse exercises.
2. Family members take turns reading from the chapter.
3. The therapist helps the family think through their own abuse dynamics.

GROUP THERAPY INSTRUCTIONS

1. The girls sit in a circle and take turns reading pages from the chapter.
2. Different girls will have undergone different patterns of abuse. These differences can be related back to the abuser strategies discussed in earlier exercises.
3. Any similarities between the girls' experiences can be used to underscore the role of the abuser versus that of the victim in the victimization.
4. The therapist should encourage positive peer support for victims.

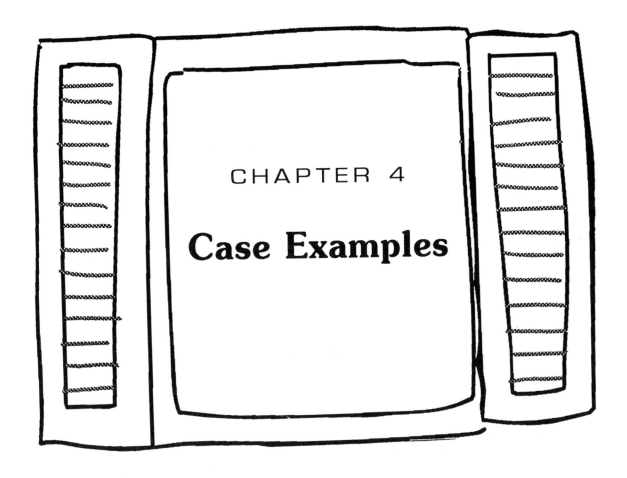

CHAPTER 4

Case Examples

Case Examples

The exercises described in Chapter 3 can be integrated into treatment sessions in many different ways depending on how key a role the exercises play in treatment. Three case examples are provided as illustrations. In the individual therapy case, the exercises played a moderately important role in introducing many treatment themes. In the family therapy case, the exercises served as the catalyst for investing family members in the treatment process; after this motivational goal had been achieved, no further exercises were used in treatment. In the group therapy case, the exercises were used to introduce all of the treatment themes covered by the group. Each case example includes a brief case history, the rationale for exercise usage, a brief discussion of how the exercise was implemented, and the short-term outcome of its implementation.*

INDIVIDUAL TREATMENT

MASTERS FAMILY

Brief Case History. Carla Masters is a 27-year-old, single parent. She has one child, Alicia (age 11). Carla did not marry, or stay long with, Alicia's father. Alicia has had no contact with her father since she was 18 months old. Until recently, Carla and Alicia have moved back and forth between several counties in the Northeast. In each county, they had resided with maternal relatives. The Masters family has never had their own home, and Carla has never had her own source of income.

Two months ago, Alicia revealed to a school teacher that her grandfather was sexually abusing her. She revealed the abuse because her grandfather was threatening to in-

---

* Names and identifying characteristics of persons in all case examples have been disguised thoroughly to protect privacy.

volve one of her younger cousins in sexual activities if Alicia did not consent to vaginal and anal intercourse. Prior to this time, the abuse had consisted of fondling and oral sex. Alicia said that her paternal uncle had also engaged her in sexual activities. She had not revealed the abuse to her mother for fear of abandonment; the perpetrators had said that Carla would desert Alicia if she found out about the abuse. Following the disclosure, the school contacted Child Protective Services, who then phoned Carla. Following this call, Carla fled the county, leaving Alicia with her grandfather. Carla's present whereabouts are unknown. Children and Youth took custody of Alicia and placed her in foster care. Children and Youth referred Alicia to treatment, focusing on her sexual victimization. On entering treatment, Alicia was friendly and verbal. Her attention span and impulse control seemed appropriate for her age.

Rationale for Exercise Implementation. Alicia had the verbal skills and intelligence to profit from direct discussion of issues not directly related to abuse; for example, how to make friends within her new school. However, any topic that related to family life or victimization sent her into a panic. Her mother had abandoned her when she revealed the abuse, just as the perpetrators had predicted. Alicia feared that if she continued to talk about the abuse her mother would never return. She idealized her mother and longed for her return. Her relationship with her foster parents had become very strained because she would plead with them to find her mother, and they would try to convince her that she was better off without Carla.

The parenting exercises were introduced to provide Alicia with the information and skill building that she needed to evaluate her relationship with her mother and her foster parents. It was considered that these issues needed to be resolved before effective work on victimization issues was possible. In the first exercise, Alicia needed to critically examine parenting scenarios from the perspective of the children's needs and the parents' responsibilities. This perspective was a very difficult one for her to assume. While she often recognized that a child was in need of something, her solution was always centered on the child's taking some specific action rather than the parent doing so. She had used this child-centered strategy within her own family. When she had seen her younger cousins in need, she had fed them, dressed them, and tried to protect them from abuse. Alicia had been the only source of positive nurturance in her family. After hearing the therapist's reactions to each scenario, she came to recognize that she and her cousins had needed to parent themselves; the adults in their family had either neglected or abused them. In the second exercise, in creating an ideal family contract, Alicia explored her idealized fantasy about her mother. In discussing this contract with the therapist, Alicia was able to articulate that implementation of this contract would require profound changes in her mother's past behavior. However, she expressed confidence that her mother would make these changes. The last exercise, in which she explored alternative living situations and the reasons for them, served as a turning point in Alicia's treatment. Alicia had a long, simulated phone conversation with her mother. She asked "Carla" why she never prepared any meals, why she never celebrated Alicia's birthdays, why she didn't protect her from her grandfather, why she had abandoned her, why she hadn't come back for her, and so on. Alicia was very tearful and intense during these conversations and reacted to the responses of the therapist as if they were Carla's responses. The conversation ended with Alicia telling "Carla" to get help learning how to be a good parent.

Outcome. Over the course of all three parenting exercises, family roles, boundaries, and responsibilities were clarified for Alicia. She came to recognize how deficient her past home environments had been. While she continued to grieve for her mother, she recognized that she was grieving for her idealized mother, not for Carla. Alicia was able to stop acting out within her foster placement and to reach out to her foster mother as an adult "mother" role model. She had gained some self-respect from recognizing how much she had done to try to care for her younger cousins. Although she realized that she could not protect them from their current situation, she could articulate that, in reporting the abuse, she had done her best to protect them. Alicia had also become able to fantasize about her life as an adult and discuss her own strategies for becoming an effective parent.

FAMILY TREATMENT

CONNORS FAMILY

Brief Case History. Cathy (age 35) and Russ (age 35) have been married for 12 years. They have two daughters, Lisa (age 11) and Karen (age 10), and two sons, Brian (age 8) and Kevin (age 6). They had one other child, Marla (deceased), who was the oldest child. The Connnors live together in a rented three-bedroom house. Russ has been unemployed for the past 3 years. He had been fired from a factory job for insubordinate behavior.

In their first 9 years of marriage, Russ was extremely physically abusive to the children. Cathy said she had tried many strategies for stopping the abuse, including reporting Russ to Children and Youth services. This report consisted of Cathy calling Children and Youth while an abusive incident was in progress. She had screamed into the phone that her children were in trouble and needed help. She had then hung up the phone and gone back to pleading with her husband to leave the children alone. The child abuse stopped abruptly 3 years ago after a family car accident in which Marla was killed; Russ had been the driver. Since this incident, Russ does not even verbally reprimand the children. He functions as their playmate. At the same time that he stopped abusing the children, he began physically and verbally abusing Cathy. He also forces her to have sexual encounters with him after physically abusive incidents.

The family entered treatment as a mandatory referral from the school system. The principal had threatened to report the parents to the authorities for neglect and expel Lisa from school if the family did not initiate treatment. Lisa has been aggressive with both teachers and peers. She also leaves the school building during the day without permission. On entering treatment, this family radiated hostility; they were furious with the therapist, the school system, and each other.

Rationale for Exercise Implementation. The family had no motivation for participating in treatment beyond avoiding further confrontations with the school system and Protective Services. The parents' attachment to each other appeared based on fears of even greater loneliness and disappointment if the marriage broke up. The children were ambivalently attached to their parents. No one could remember any past examples of supportive family interactions. No one expressed any hope that positive changes could occur in their current family relationships.

The exercises on recognition and expression of feelings were introduced early in treatment. The initial goals for these exercises were to teach the family the skills necessary to recognize and express other feelings besides rage and to give the family opportunities to have fun experiences where they could experience positive parent-parent and parent-child interactions.

During the first phase of "Feeling Word Charades," when individual family members acted out feelings alone, the children did well, but the parents passively resisted. A turning point occurred when family members were asked to work in teams of two to act out feelings. The 6-year-old son, Kevin, asked his father for help. The father told him to ask someone else. Cathy intervened by insisting that Russ help out. Russ responded by telling her that she should go help the boy herself. Russ then began to systematically ridicule Cathy's attempts to help the child. The therapist intervened. She took the mother and child into a corner to help them brainstorm how they could act out their word. The therapist praised the mother for coming forward to help the 6-year-old. The word this mother-son team was supposed to act out was "silly." They decided to express this feeling by dancing and jumping around the room together. Lisa guessed "silly" immediately. The rest of the family responded to Lisa's success with ridicule. The therapist cut off the verbal abuse by labeling it sour grapes and challenging the next team to surpass the Cathy-Kevin-Lisa triumph. By the end of this session, the family was working well together in two-person teams. Everyone, with the exception of the father, seemed to have enjoyed the session activity. In the next session, family members were assigned to work together in progressively larger teams. Russ was very creative in developing scenarios to act out his assigned feelings. The children were honestly impressed by his abilities. In addition, they were having a great time being part of his teams. Another turning point occurred when the therapist admitted to intentionally giving the father the most difficult feelings to act out. The therapist praised Russ for both his creativity and his positive parenting while orchestrating his scenarios. Russ felt the genuineness of these comments and began to smile. His children encouraged him to be in charge of the last word to be acted out that session. Russ even included Cathy in this last effort - leaving only the therapist to serve as the audience.

Outcome. The Connors completed only the "Feeling Word Charades" exercise of the feeling expression and recognition unit. However, through working through various permutations of this exercise, the parents shifted their perception of what family life could be. Cathy and Russ had previously been resigned to their marriage and their role as parents. Now they had experienced a sense of satisfaction from helping their children and had actually enjoyed spending time with them. Cathy and Russ came to be hopeful that therapy could in fact do more for them than keep the school from expelling Lisa. This led them to agree to participate in marital as well as family sessions.

GROUP TREATMENT

DALTON FAMILY

Brief Case History. Elaine (age 32) and Larry (age 38) have been married for 14 years. They have two children, Laura (age 12) and Kevin (age 8). Elaine, Larry, and Laura live together in a two-bedroom trailer that frequently lacks heat and running water. Kevin lives across the street with his grandparents. Larry is employed on a local farm at minimum wage. He often spends his paycheck at a local bar before coming home.

Elaine, Larry, and the children have had erratic contacts over the last 10 years with the community mental health system. Both parents have been diagnosed as schizophrenic and periodically take psychotropic medication. Their parenting skills fluctuate along with their medication use. When doing well, they can provide basic minimal physical care and somewhat neglectful psychological care. When the parents are decompensating, they are physically and psychologically abusive and neglectful. The children have never received routine medical or dental care.

Two months ago, a police cruiser found Laura walking along the berm of the highway. She was disheveled and incoherent. She relayed later to a Child Protective Services (CPS) worker that she had been left home alone with a teenage neighbor, and he had raped her at knife point. Child Protective Services returned her to her parents but took legal custody of her. They told Elaine and Larry that Laura would stay in their home only if she received treatment services. Child Protective Services made weekly contacts with the Daltons to check on the physical care the children were receiving and to transport Laura to a community mental health center. Laura was referred to a therapy group for preteen girls. It was a structured, insight-oriented group in which a skill-building exercise served as the core component of each session. During the initial sessions, Laura was verbally abusive to the group leaders and verbally and physically assaultive to her peers. Her pattern was to instigate fights or run out of the room whenever she was not the focus of the group's attention.

Rationale for Exercise Implementation. Laura's neglectful upbringing had inhibited her development of age-appropriate self-control and social skills; however, it had not inhibited her desire for peer acceptance. The therapists had noted that despite her hostile behavior toward peers, their opinions of her seemed to carry more weight than that of the adults. The exercises on developing constructive peer relationships were implemented. It was hoped that two goals would be achieved. One, that Laura's intrinsic interest in peers would provide her with the motivation to respond constructively to these exercises, and two, that Laura's mastery of the skills within this unit would lead her to behave constructively toward group members. In the first exercise, the girls worked to generate lists of the characteristics of good and bad friends. Laura was relatively quiet. However, she disagreed with the group when they said that a good friend was never verbally or physically aggressive. During the second exercise, when the girls were instructed to act out the friendship scenarios, Laura volunteered to be the aggressor in a scenario that involved a "bad" friend. Instead, the group leader assigned her to scenarios in which she characterized a "good" friend. In one of these scenarios, Laura helped another girl work through a family fight. In another, she helped a girl who was having trouble in school. Laura took her roles in these scenarios very seriously. She beamed when her character was praised by other girls as representing a "good" friend. After this experience, Laura experienced a shift in her sense of personal identity. She seemed to have absorbed the values of the two "good friends" she had acted out into her own sense of self. For example, she made conscious, and sometimes heavy-handed, attempts to be empathetic and helpful to other group members. When the attention of the group was on someone else's problem, she still tried to shift the focus to herself. However, she was now doing it from the perspective of being the emotional supporter or master advice giver to whoever was in distress rather than acting out. In addition, because one of her characters had cared about school, Laura began completing her schoolwork; she now identified herself as someone who cared about school.

Outcome. Participating in the exercises on peer relationships served as a turning point in Laura's treatment through providing her with the personal motivation to gain control over her own behavior. She was motivated to change because she understood the difference between how she had behaved in the past and good-friend behavior. She developed a more positive sense of herself and actively tried to use the skills learned in these exercises to develop friendships with the other girls in group. Now that her acting-out behavior was under control, she profited from other group exercises. The next exercises that had a noticeable impact on Laura were those in the sexuality unit. Due to lack of parenting and lack of hot water, Laura had often been unkempt. After the body-image exercises, Laura began to come early to her therapy sessions and wash her face and hair in the hot water in the bathroom. While this often meant she came to group literally dripping wet, the group supported her attempts at dealing constructively with her body. After the exercises on puberty, Laura realized that she was more fully developed than most of the other girls in group. She experienced a sense of pride over this and never lost an opportunity to remind group members of it. The leaders insisted that she earn this "high status" by being a role model for maturity. Laura did attempt to be a role model within, as well as outside of, group. For example, she began to encourage her younger brother to bathe, do his homework, and so on. The exercises on parenting helped Laura develop insight into what was and was not under her control within the family and to engender hope that, as an adult, she could become part of a family that was emotionally supportive.

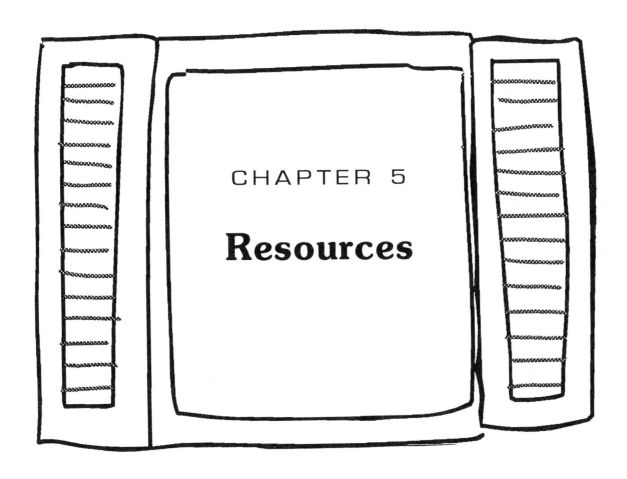

CHAPTER 5

Resources

Resources

Beckford, P., & Berman, P. (1992). Impact of witnessing parental violence on adult children. Unpublished doctoral dissertation, Indiana University of Pennsylvania, Indiana, Pennsylvania.

Berman, P. (1993). Impact of abusive marital relationships on children. In M. Hansen & M. Harway (Eds.), *Battering and Family Therapy: A Feminist Family Therapy Perspective.* Newbury Park, CA: Sage.

Berman, P. (1992). Group treatment for sexually abused preteen girls. In L. VandeCreek, S. Knapp, & T. L. Jackson (Eds.), *Innovations in Clinical Practice: A Source Book* (Vol. 11, pp. 109-122). Sarasota, FL: Professional Resource Press.

Berman, P. (1990). Group therapy techniques for sexually abused preteen girls. *Child Welfare, 69,* 239-252.

Channing L. Bete Co., Inc. (1989). *About Child Abuse.* Available from Channing L. Bete Co., Inc., 200 State Road, South Deerfield, MA 01373. Telephone: (800) 628-7733.

Channing L. Bete Co., Inc. (1979). *About Wife Abuse.* Available from Channing L. Bete Co., Inc., 200 State Road, South Deerfield, MA 01373. Telephone: (800) 628-7733.

Daugherty, L. (1984). *Why Me? Help for Victims of Child Sexual Abuse.* (Chapters 1-2, pp. 11-28). Racine, WI: Mother Courage Press.

Erikson, E. (1963). *Childhood and Society.* New York: W.W. Norton.

Eron, L. (1987). The development of aggressive behavior from the perspective of a developing behaviorism. *American Psychologist, 42,* 435-442.

Garbarino, J., Kostelny, K., & Dubrow, N. (1991). What children can tell us about living in danger. *American Psychologist, 46,* 376-383.

Gordon, S. (1981). *The Teenage Survival Book.* New York: Random House.

Gordon, T. (1975). *Parent Effectiveness Training.* New York: Plume Books.

Gruszenski, R., Brink, J., & Edleson, J. (1988). Support and education groups for children of battered women. *Child Welfare, 67,* 431-444.

Jaffe, P., Wolfe, D., & Wilson, S. (1990). *Children of Battered Women*. Newbury Park, CA: Sage.

Karpel, M., & Strauss, E. (1983). *Family Evaluation* (Chapter 11, pp. 245-262). New York: Gardner.

Koestner, R., Weinberger, J., & Franz, C. (1990). The family origins of empathetic concern: A 26-year longitudinal study. *Journal of Personality and Social Psychology, 58*, 709-717.

Lange, A., & Jakubowski, P. (1976). *Responsible Assertive Behavior*. Champaign, IL: Research Press.

Mayle, P. (1975). *What's Happening to Me?* Secaucus, NJ: Lyle Stuart.

Mischley, M., Mischley, L., & Ingold, B. (1983). *Parent Education for Low Income Families with Young Children*. Lansing: Michigan Department of Mental Health.

Sgroi, S. (1985). *Handbook of Clinical Intervention in Child Sexual Abuse*. Lexington, KY: Lexington Books.

Swink, K., & Leveille, E. (1986). From victim to survivor: A new look at the issues and recovery process for adult incest survivors. In D. Howard (Ed.), *A Guide to Dynamics of Feminist Therapy* (pp. 119-141). New York: Haworth.

U.S. Department of Health and Human Services, Office of Human Development Services. (1980). *Adolescent Abuse and Neglect: Intervention Strategies* (OHDS 80-30266). Washington, DC: U.S. Government Printing Office.

U.S. Department of Health and Human Services, Office of Human Development Services. (1988). *Executive Summary: Study of National Incidence and Prevalence of Child Abuse and Neglect*. Contract 105-85-1702. Washington, DC: Clearinghouse on Child Abuse and Neglect Information.

U.S. Department of Health and Human Services, Office of Human Development Services. (1989). *Child Abuse and Neglect: A Shared Community Concern*. Washington, DC: Clearinghouse on Child Abuse and Neglect Information.

Wachter, O. (1983). *No More Secrets for Me*. Boston: Little, Brown.

APPENDIX

You Sparkle: A Handbook for Girls

How To Use This Handbook

The *Handbook for Girls* is designed to be copied and distributed as a resource for preteen and teenage girls. It is intended to increase the long-term impact of individual, family, or group treatment that has followed the skill-building units covered in Chapter 3. Optimally, this handbook can be given to a girl when she is ready to terminate treatment. Each page of the handbook can be read aloud and discussed within a therapy session. As treatment themes are reviewed, the therapist can encourage a discussion of the girl's progress. Girls can be encouraged to look through the handbook whenever they miss being in therapy or whenever they have a problem and aren't sure what to do. If a girl is withdrawn prematurely from treatment, the handbook can be sent to her or given to her via a Child Protective Service caseworker.

Each copy of the handbook needs to be individualized for a specific girl by putting the correct phone numbers on the page entitled "Do You Have a Problem" and by the therapist signing the last page. Do *not* copy this page when you prepare *You Sparkle: A Handbook for Girls* for distribution to the girls. Begin copying with the title page on A-1.

The handbook will not be appropriate for girls who have significant reading difficulties.

You Sparkle: A Handbook for Girls

Table of Contents

WHO ARE YOU?

YOU SPARKLE!

1. You are very special and important because:

   a. no one looks exactly like you.
   b. no one talks or laughs exactly like you.
   c. no one thinks exactly like you.

2. You are very likable and lovable and:

   a. there are many people in this world who will want to be your friends once they know what you are really like.
   b. there are many adults who will want to care for you and help you when they know what you are really like.

NOT EVERY PERSON WILL RECOGNIZE THAT YOU SPARKLE

1. This is because every person is different and not everyone will like the same things you do.
2. This is because it is not easy to understand another person.
3. This is because not everyone takes the time they need to get to know someone.

YOU WILL ALWAYS SPARKLE!

1. You are the most important person who needs to remember this! ! ! !
2. You may need to help others realize this! ! ! !

HOW DO YOU FEEL?

RECOGNIZING AND UNDERSTANDING
THAT FEELINGS ARE IMPORTANT

1. Everyone has feelings. Feelings are never stupid; they are always very important.
2. Learning to identify different feelings in yourself and other people can be hard and takes practice.

   Examples of Feelings: Happy, Love, Silly, Proud, Curious, Excited, Bored, Guilty, Angry, Sad, Tired, Lonely, Sorry, Scared, Jealous, Pain, Worried, Frustrated, Embarrassed, Hungry, Surprised, Restless.

3. Not everyone will feel the same way about things as you do. It is important to respect other people's feelings even when they are different from yours.

   Example: Cathy's mom is sitting alone and staring out of the window. Cathy comes home very excited about her report card. Cathy starts to tell her mom but Mom screams at Cathy to go away. Cathy tries again to talk to her mom. Mom grabs Cathy by the arm and screams and screams and screams.

   a. Cathy might feel sad that this happened and think that her mom didn't care about her report card.
   b. Cathy might feel angry that this happened and think that her mom was cruel.
   c. Cathy might feel scared that this happened and wonder if Mom was going to hurt her.
   d. Cathy might feel worried that this happened and wonder what was wrong with her mom.

   There are many other feelings you might have if this had happened to you. There is no right or wrong way to feel. It is important for everyone to learn to recognize and understand their own feelings.
4. It's okay to be angry, or sad, or jealous. Everyone feels that way sometimes. But express these feelings assertively - don't be cruel.
5. Talking about your feelings - both the nice ones (Love, Happy, Silly) and the not-so-nice ones (Sad, Angry, Jealous) - is a good way to become close to a member of your family or to friends. Always try to express your feelings in an assertive and self-confident way.
6. If you are scared or puzzled by your feelings, or if you don't know how to express them in an assertive way, ask for advice from someone you trust.

WHAT IS ASSERTIVENESS?

STAND UP FOR YOURSELF AND RESPECT OTHERS

1. Being assertive means standing up for yourself and expressing your feelings in a way that doesn't blame other people or push them around.
2. Being assertive doesn't mean people will always be nice to you or listen to what you say. However, being assertive is the best way to try to get someone to be nice and listen to what you say.

Examples of How To Be Assertive

a. Your best friend has called you a bad name.

   Assertive: I feel hurt that you are calling me names.

b. Your mother always sends you to your room whenever you get home from school; you would like to talk with her.

   Assertive: I feel disappointed when you send me to my room because I would like to talk with you.

c. Your friend always wants to play basketball and you don't like basketball.

   Assertive: I really like you, but I don't like to play basketball.

3. Being assertive means you never threaten or try to push other people to do what they don't want to do.

   Don't Say: If you don't do it, I won't be your friend.

4. Saying something in an assertive way means you state your true feelings and why you feel that way.

   Assertive: I feel (feeling) happy (why) because you remembered my birthday.

   Assertive: I feel (feeling) jealous (why) because you are spending time with someone else.

5. It can be hard to be assertive, especially if you are angry - but always try. If you make a mistake and say something in a mean way, apologize in an assertive manner.

Assertive: I am sorry that I swore at you. I was feeling really angry because you said I had to wash dishes and I hate washing dishes.

WHAT IS A FRIEND?

WHO IS A FRIEND?

1. A good friend is:

    a. someone who likes you.
    b. someone you can talk to.
    c. someone you can have fun with.
    d. BUT, THERE ARE DIFFERENT TYPES OF FRIENDS.

WHO IS A GOOD FRIEND?

1. Good friends really care about you and:

    a. will listen to your feelings and will not make fun of them.
    b. will never intentionally hurt you even if they hurt you accidentally.
    c. will be considerate of what you like and don't like, and will compromise with you.

2. Good friends encourage you to do constructive things (things that are good for you) and:

    a. help you if you are in trouble even if they are busy or mad at you.
    b. encourage you to face your problems no matter how scary the problems are.
    c. tell you the truth and help you tell the truth.
    d. talk to you after having a fight with you and remain your friend.
    e. keep your secrets unless it will help you if they tell someone.

WHO IS A BAD FRIEND?

1. Bad friends don't really care about you and:

    a. hurt your feelings intentionally.
    b. say cruel things about you behind your back but may be nice to you when you meet face to face.
    c. lie about you.
    d. tell your secrets when they are mad at you.

2. Bad friends take advantage of you and:

    a. threaten not to be your friend if you don't do what they want.
    b. borrow your things without asking or won't return your things when you ask them to.

c. break a rule and let you take the blame.

d. say nice things to you just to get you to do their homework or give them your money.

e. lie to you or encourage you to lie to keep out of trouble.

f. abuse your body.

3. Bad friends encourage you to be self-destructive by doing things which cause you harm and:

a. encourage you to cut class because you don't like the teacher.

b. encourage you to drink alcohol or take drugs when you are lonely or sad.

c. suggest that you run away from home when you are fighting with your parents.

d. suggest you steal something when you want it but have no money to buy it.

e. encourage you to be mean to someone else when you feel sad or mad.

CHOOSE TO BE A GOOD FRIEND

1. **A Friendship Example:** You've just had a fight with your mom and have run over to a friend's house. Your friend listens to you talk about how you feel.

   a. *A Good Friend:* This person helps you figure out what to say to your mom when you go home, and walks back to your house with you as moral support.

   b. *A Bad Friend:* This person invites you to spend the night at her house and promises to hide you from your mother.

2. **Conclusions**

   a. Both kinds of friends try to help you, but a bad friend just gets you into more trouble rather than really helping.

   b. Nobody is perfect. Everyone should try to be a good friend but everyone makes mistakes. If you are a bad friend to someone - it's okay - just apologize in an assertive way and keep trying to be a good friend.

WHAT IS A GOOD DATE?

Most dates seem cute, fun, and exciting. However, some are good and some are bad dates.

WHO IS A GOOD DATE?

1. Someone who:

    a. likes you exactly the way you are.
    b. respects your thoughts and feelings.
    c. is always honest with you.
    d. cares about you when you are sick.
    e. cares about what you like to do.
    f. won't drink alcohol or take drugs.
    g. wouldn't hit you.
    h. is polite to your family and friends.

WHO IS A BAD DATE?

1. Someone who:

    a. might lie to you.
    b. might scare you or hit you.
    c. might make fun of your thoughts or feelings.
    d. might try to force you to do things you don't want to do.
    e. might steal, drink, or take drugs.
    f. might be rude to your family and friends.
    g. might encourage you to skip school or neglect your homework.

Sometimes dates can seem strange and confusing; however, always remember that they have feelings, too. Girls who sparkle always try to respect the feelings and thoughts of other people. If your date does some of the things that bad dates do, talk assertively about it. It's hard to be a good date. Both you and your date may make mistakes - it's okay; everybody does.

HOW DO YOU BEGIN A GOOD RELATIONSHIP?

BE A GOOD DATE

1. Do be assertive and be yourself by:

   a. smiling.
   b. talking about something you have in common such as school, homework, and movies.
   c. acting like you normally do.
   d. wearing clean clothes.
   e. practicing good grooming.

DON'T BE A BAD DATE

1. Don't put yourself down to make them feel good.
2. Don't act sexy by:

   a. walking in a "slinky" way.
   b. wearing clothes that are too tight.
   c. wearing really low-cut blouses or unbuttoning your blouse.
   d. not wearing a bra.
   e. wearing shoes with really high heels.
   f. talking like you have a lot of sexual experience.
   g. wearing too much makeup.

3. Don't lie about your age or about your life to seem cool.
4. Don't smoke, drink, or take drugs.
5. Don't say insulting "smart" comments to get their attention.

A good romantic relationship develops between two people who like and respect themselves as well as each other. If someone is being abused or taken advantage of, it is not a good relationship.

HOW DO YOU FEEL ABOUT YOUR BODY?

YOUR BODY IS CHANGING

1. Young people go through many physical changes as they grow older.
2. Young people may or may not know that these physical changes are going to happen or what they mean.

   Example: Nancy has just begun her first menstrual period. She doesn't know why she is bleeding. When her mother found her, Nancy was in the basement, behind the washing machine. Nancy's mother told her to go upstairs. Later that day, Nancy's mom threw a box of tampons on Nancy's lap and then walked away.

   a. Nancy might feel angry that her mother did not provide her with more help.
   b. Nancy might feel disgusted with her body.
   c. Nancy might be afraid that she was going to die.
   d. Nancy might. . . .

YOUR FEELINGS ABOUT OTHERS ARE CHANGING

1. Young people begin to feel sexually attracted to others as they grow older.
2. Young people may or may not receive any help in understanding these feelings and what they do and do not represent.

   Example: A really attractive person walked by. Sarah blushed and felt a surge of excitement. Sarah found herself fantasizing about being touched by this person.

   a. Sarah might think she is in love with this person.
   b. Sarah might hate herself for having these feelings.
   c. Sarah might be ashamed of these feelings.
   d. Sarah might. . . .

YOUR BODY BELONGS TO YOU

1. Young people may not feel in control of their own bodies.

   Example: Ruth's father and uncle have engaged her in sexual activities for as long as she can remember. After going through puberty, Ruth began to understand what these sexual contacts represented.

a. Ruth might begin to have sexual contacts with peers.

b. Ruth might feel disgusted when anyone touched her body.

c. Ruth might begin to mutilate her body.

d. Ruth might. . . .

2. Young people have a right to control their own bodies and feel proud of the changes their bodies are going through.

3. Sexual feelings can be confusing, especially because you can be sexually attracted to strangers, people you do not like, and people who don't like you, as well as people you love.

It is okay to need time and help in understanding how to take good care of your body and deal constructively with sexual feelings.

DO YOU HAVE A PROBLEM?

WHEN YOU HAVE A PROBLEM, TALK TO SOMEONE YOU CAN TRUST

1. Phone numbers of people you can trust (e.g., friends, family, teachers, family doctor, police department, Children's Protective Services, Community Mental Health Center, Crisis Line):

__Name__	__Phone Number__
_____	_____
_____	_____
_____	_____
_____	_____
_____	_____
_____	_____
_____	_____
_____	_____
_____	_____
_____	_____

2. If you tell someone and that person does not help you, tell someone else.
3. If the problem is really big, you may need to talk to and get help from more than one person.

BIG PROBLEMS WILL NEVER GO AWAY IF YOU IGNORE THEM

1. Talking about problems is the best first step in making them go away.
2. It may hurt to talk about your problems, but it will always hurt you more if you hide your problems and just hope they will go away.
3. The bigger the problem is, the more you have to talk and think about it before the problem goes away.

WHAT IS NEGLECT?

CHILDREN NEED CARE

1. When parents do not provide children with appropriate physical, emotional, or developmental care, it is called *NEGLECT*.
2. Parents are supposed to take care of their children's physical needs by providing their children with:

    a. healthy food to eat.
    b. a safe place to live.
    c. protective clothing (warm in cold weather, light in warm weather).
    d. medical and dental care to keep their bodies healthy.
    e. safety from danger (examples: car accidents, drug abuse, sexual abuse, violence).

3. Parents are supposed to take care of their children's emotional needs by:

    a. playing with their children.
    b. being physically affectionate by appropriate (not sexual) touching.
    c. being verbally affectionate by appropriate praise and recognition of their children's special qualities.
    d. helping their children make friends with other children.
    e. helping their children get along with other adults.

4. Parents are supposed to take care of their children's developmental needs by:

    a. teaching them how to be physically independent (examples: how to wash, dress, clean their teeth, eat properly).
    b. teaching them how to be emotionally independent (examples: recognize, understand and express their feelings, solve problems).
    c. teaching them how to have self-control (examples: follow rules, take turns, be patient).

PARENTS NEED MANY SKILLS

1. Many adults have children without thinking through how difficult it can be to take good care of children.
2. Many adults did not have good parenting themselves and so do not know what they need to do to take good care of children.
3. Some adults have children without considering that they may not want to do all the things that are necessary to provide good care for children.

NEGLECT MUST STOP

1. Children are not responsible for the kind of parenting they receive.
2. Adults are responsible for the welfare of children.

    a. If you are being neglected by your parents, other adults should be contacted for help. These other adults can include other adult family members, Child Protective Service workers, police officers, teachers, doctors, and therapists.

    b. If the neglect does not stop, keep telling other adults until you get the help you need.

WHAT IS SPOUSAL VIOLENCE?

ADULTS MAY ATTACK EACH OTHER

1. When husbands and wives (or other adults living together) physically hurt each other, this is called spousal violence.
2. While wives and husbands can both engage in violent behavior, the violence usually begins with husbands attacking wives.
3. Violence often begins as verbal abuse, pushing, or shoving.
4. Violence usually increases in frequency and level of dangerousness and can include:

   a. hitting.
   b. kicking.
   c. biting.
   d. assault with objects.
   e. assault with a weapon.
   f. murder.

YOUNG PEOPLE ARE SEEING SPOUSAL VIOLENCE

1. Young people may think:

   a. my mom or dad might get hurt.
   b. I don't know what to do.
   c. I'm so tired of all this.
   d. I'm too scared to think.
   e. my mom (dad) deserves this.
   f. I need to protect myself.
   g. I wish I could hit her (him) too.
   h. I need to stop them.

2. Young people may feel:

   a. sad.
   b. sick.
   c. indifferent.
   d. mad.
   e. scared.
   f. numb.

3. Young people may react to the violence by:

    a. trying to stop it (yelling at parents, pleading, trying to distract them, calling for help).
    b. withdrawing from it (crying, running away, hiding, trying to hurt themselves).
    c. aggressing against others (threatening, hitting, kicking).

4. At home, school, and with peers young people may:

    a. try to be very responsible, take care of others, excel.
    b. act younger than they are, spend a lot of time alone, underachieve.
    c. act tough, defy authority, bully peers, underachieve.

SPOUSAL VIOLENCE MUST STOP

1. It is the responsibility of adults to stop family violence.
2. If there is violence in your home, talk to an adult you trust about it.
3. If the violence is not stopped, keep telling other people until you get the help you need.

WHAT IS PHYSICAL ABUSE?

ADULTS MAY ATTACK YOUNG PEOPLE

1. If someone has intentionally bruised, scraped, burned, cut, or poked a hole in a person's body, this person has been physically abused. No one has the right to do this to anyone.
2. Many young people have been physically abused.

YOUNG PEOPLE MAKE MISTAKES

1. Many young people have done things that are wrong, such as:

   a. lying.
   b. stealing.
   c. fighting.
   d. yelling.
   e. refusing to do homework.
   f. refusing to do chores.

2. No one should physically abuse young people even if you have done all of these things. Some people are physically abused even though they have not done any of these things.

PHYSICAL ABUSE MUST STOP

1. If someone is physically abusing you, tell an adult that you trust.
2. If the abuse is not stopped, keep telling other people until you get the help you need.

WHAT IS SEXUAL ABUSE?

WHO ARE THE ABUSERS?

1. Sexual abusers are adults, or individuals at least 5 years older than a young person, who engage the young person in sexual activities. Sexual abuse can include watching or making pornographic movies or pictures; fondling the young person's genitals or breasts; exhibitionism; oral, anal, or vaginal intercourse; and other forms of sexual exploitation.
2. Sexual abusers have serious psychological problems and are sexually attracted to young people. Abusers may involve younger family members in sex or exploit other young people they come in contact with.
3. Some sexual abusers use gifts or fun activities to make young people feel as if they cooperated or wanted to engage in sexual acts. Other sexual abusers use verbal or physical threats to make young people engage in sexual acts.

WHO ARE THE YOUNG PEOPLE?

1. Many boys and girls have been sexually abused. The abuse may have started in infancy, childhood, or in the teen years.
2. Young people who have been sexually abused often feel guilty and sad because they think the abuse was their fault. Even when a young person thought they cooperated, the abuse was still the older person's fault.
3. Young people may feel confused because, when the older person touched them sexually, it felt good and not uncomfortable. This is not unusual. The abuser was still at fault and should not have been engaging the young person in sexual activity.
4. Young people may feel sad, angry, helpless, or disgusted when the older person touches them sexually. The abuser has no right to engage the young person in sexual activity.

SEXUAL ABUSE MUST STOP

1. Young people have a right to control their own bodies.
2. If someone is sexually abusing you, tell an adult that you trust.
3. If the abuse is not stopped, keep telling other people until you get the help you need.

WHAT ARE YOUR GOALS?

BE A GOOD FRIEND TO YOURSELF
(LIKE YOURSELF, LIKE YOUR BODY) BY:

1. recognizing and understanding your feelings.
2. being assertive in expressing your thoughts and feelings.
3. talking about your problems.
4. being honest.

BE A GOOD FRIEND TO OTHERS BY:

1. recognizing and trying to understand their feelings, even if these feelings are very different from yours.
2. encouraging your friends who have problems to talk about their problems with an adult.
3. helping them to tell an adult they trust if they have a scary secret.

HOW DO YOU SAY GOODBYE?

WHY DO FRIENDS SAY GOODBYE?

1. If a friend says goodbye, it is not because he or she doesn't like you.
2. Sometimes you have to say goodbye to a friend because you are moving far away.
3. Sometimes you have to say goodbye to a friend because he or she is moving away.

   a. Saying goodbye to someone you like can be very hard. You may feel sad, angry, or confused. That's okay. It can be hard, but try to express your thoughts and feelings in an assertive way when you say goodbye.

4. You can still be a friend to someone even if you don't see him or her for a long time - even if you never see him or her again.
5. If you miss a friend, try to remember some fun times or bad times that you had with your friend. This will help you feel close to him or her again.
6. If you are lonely for your friend, talk to someone you can trust about it.
7. If you are having trouble making new friends, look through this handbook and remember all the things you have learned that could help you make friends.

REMEMBER THAT TO MAKE FRIENDS YOU SHOULD:

1. Feel good about yourself. You sparkle and are full of special thoughts and feelings (see "Who Are You" on page A-3).
2. Be assertive when you deal with others. Go up to people who look nice and ask them if they would like to talk or do some activity with you (see "What Is Assertiveness" on pages A-7 to A-8).
3. Think carefully about whether you and the person you are with are trying to be good friends (see "What Is a Friend" on pages A-9 to A-10).
4. Don't give up. Some people whom you like may not like you. That's okay, it happens to everyone! ! ! Always remember you sparkle. If one person you ask won't spend time with you, ask someone else! ! ! !

GOODBYE SPARKLING ONE! ! !

YOU WILL ALWAYS BE MY

FRIEND! ! ! !

_____

Therapist's Signature

If You Found This Book Useful . . .

You might want to know more about our other titles.

For a complete listing of our publications, please write, call, or fax the following information. You may fold this sheet to make a postpaid reply envelope.

Name _____

(Please Print)

Institution/Company _____

Address _____

Address _____

City/State/Zip _____

I am a (check one):

❑ psychologist   ❑ school psychologist
❑ clinical social worker   ❑ psychiatrist
❑ marriage and family therapist   ❑ other: _____
❑ mental health counselor

↓ Fold Here To Mail ↓   ↓ Fold Here To Mail ↓

To order additional copies of *Therapeutic Exercises for Victimized and Neglected Girls: Applications for Individual, Family, and Group Psychotherapy*, please complete the section below:

Send _____ copies of *Therapeutic Exercises for Victimized and Neglected Girls: Applications for Individual, Family, and Group Psychotherapy*. Price: $28.20 U.S.; $30.20 Foreign (includes shipping). Florida residents add $1.75 sales tax.

❑ Check enclosed   ❑ Charge my (circle one):   Visa   MasterCard   American Express   Discover

Card # _____ Expiration Date _____

Signature _____

Daytime Telephone Number (_____) _____

❑ Ship to (please print):

Name _____

Address _____

Address _____

City/State/Zip _____

Thank You!

Professional Resource Press • P.O. Box 15560 • Sarasota, FL 34277-1560
Telephone 813-366-7913 • Fax 813-366-7971

↓ Tape On This Edge (DO NOT STAPLE) ↓

Add A Colleague To Our Mailing List . . .

If you would like us to send our latest catalog to one of your colleagues, please return the form below:

Name _____
(Please Print)

Address_____

Address_____

City/State/Zip_____

This person is a (check one):

❑ psychologist   ❑ marriage and family therapist   ❑ school psychologist
❑ clinical social worker   ❑ mental health counselor   ❑ psychiatrist
❑ other: _____

↓ Fold Here, Tape (DO NOT STAPLE), and Mail ↓

NO POSTAGE
NECESSARY
IF MAILED
IN THE
UNITED STATES

BUSINESS   REPLY   MAIL
FIRST-CLASS MAIL   PERMIT NO 445   SARASOTA FL

POSTAGE WILL BE PAID BY ADDRESSEE

PROFESSIONAL RESOURCE PRESS
PO BOX 15560
SARASOTA FL 34277-9900